Topsy Turvy

By Charles Giuliano

Images by Charles Giuliano and,
when indicated, by Astrid Hiemer.

Berkshire Fine Arts, LLC
North Adams, Massachusetts

berkshirefinearts.com

For Astrid Hiemer, who has shared a rich and vivid life through the arts, my love and thanks for her continual support of the poetry project.

Contents

People 121

META 153

High Bush

By Charles Giuliano

Many people have a book in them.

There is value in our life and an urge to share insights and experiences.

The memoirs of celebrities, often "as told to," or biographies authorized and not, have a broad appeal to readers.

The efforts of the less well known, poor, and obscure, attract little or no attention.

One might argue the humanist position that no life is without value and significance.

At the trial resulting in execution, Socrates stated, "The unexamined life is not worth living."

This is my fifth book resulting from reflection and introspection.

With each subsequent volume the challenge has become ever more difficult.

Initially, as a result of a privileged life in the arts, there has been rich material to draw upon. With the gift of gab from my Irish heritage conflated with Sicilian audacity there have been compelling encounters, experiences, and anecdotes to set down in staccato, gonzo verse. As an inventor of literary form I had no rules to follow.

There have been no mentors and masters, although family and friends have been generous with responses and comments. My wife, Astrid, is always the first reader and discussant. Ultimately, however, we pass through a life in art naked, screaming, and mostly alone. It is why we so value our lovers. They get us through long, hard nights, and bleak, cold winters.

Things always look better in the light of morning when the straw has been spun to gold.

The work has followed its own path catapulting and caterwauling forward in a lewd and raucous manner. Many of the poems froze in final form tales and anecdotes that have been told over and over. Perhaps those who have heard them too often urge one to let them go.

How often are we bored to hear the same old stories from our friends? Part of the pleasure of new acquaintances is the opportunity to dust them off for a fresh audience.

There is a need for new experiences, adventures, and insights. By a fifth book, arguably, the obvious tropes of youth, family, friends, travel, and encounters through the arts are tapped out. There is only so much oil meant to light lamps for a week.

As my literary consigliore, Robert Henriquez, essayist and

friend asks "What happens after you have harvested the low hanging fruit? Then you have to climb higher on the bush."

Things happen during that ascent. The air gets colder, crisper, and ever more thin. It is harder to breathe and maintain the pace. There are no obvious markers and it is easy to ramble off and get lost in a thicket. When exploring with no map it's easy to get confused. Things don't work. The triage of editing gets ever more harsh and brutal. There is a heightened sense of confusion and failure.

Ever more experimental, one wonders if there will be an audience for these efforts. What's the hook to market and sell to a reader?

But isn't that precisely the commonality of all new work? The challenges are daunting, doubts riveting, but rewards, however incremental, are unprecedented. There is the comforting notion that easy and popular art doesn't last long.

It is entirely possible that something that burst out of an artist, initially raw and unknowable, the product of passion and instinct, may mean something to a stranger. The true audience is someone unknown, perhaps from another time and place.

To be or not to be.

There is a conceit that keeps us going. This new book, now the fifth, more difficult and perverse, an arrogance of verse, is arguably the best. If we don't believe it, there is no point to the effort.

It is through risk, adventure, and experimentation when we are true to ourselves and take shape as artists.

This is what's worth examining in a life. A part of that is creative monasticism, abandoning the material world in pursuit of our own meaning and spirituality.

Come with me, please, through this terra incognita up the river in search of Kurtz.

Out and About

Rockport Harbor.

View of Mt. Greylock from Adams.

Steeple Town Minus One

This is the church
This is the steeple
Open the door
See all the people
Children's hand game
Once booming North Adams
Rich on King Cotton
Mills spinning
From thread to cloth
Arnold Print Works
Vast campus once Sprague Electric
Now MASS MoCA
They worshiped
French, Irish, Polish
Churches for each
Catholic and Protestant
Steeples dominating skyline
Fallen on hard times
Jobs long gone
Some churches shuttered
Converted to museums
Others lay vacant
Pious logos
SteepleCats local ball team
Restaurant and realty
Proud of its spires
Now one less
Demolished hundred-year-old
St. Francis of Assisi
Safety hazard
Keeping the bells

For whom will they toll
Calling no faithful
To worship change

This church was razed in Steeple Town, North Adams.

Sushi House

Weekly gathering
Artists and friends
Remembering Sushi House
Heart of North Adams
Dead of winter
Just a few little as two
Intimate evenings
Braving the cold
Tales of bears
In local backyards
Hunkered down while
Snowbirds
Friends and neighbors
Gone for now
Mostly Florida
Mar y Sol
Walking the beach
Months in Mexico
Affordable Portugal
Where Astrid wants
To go next winter
No more toughing it out
Joy taking orders
Starting with margaritas
Then clash and clatter
Clang on a glass when
Strays fly back
Tables added
Heady cacophony
Change in the air
Not just a name

Ming's Pan Asian
Will it be the same
Those who came and went
Their money spent
Anticipating a new
Feng shui

Pagoda.

Greylock Greenhouses

Danger of frost now passed
Safe to plant come Memorial Day
Greenhouses on Greylock Mountain
Annual visit now less ambitious
Cutting back no tomatoes
Just planting zinnias
Some snapdragons
Mild winter he said
Resuming annual conversation
Killed the orchard though
March too warm then
April so friggin' cold
Lost half the orchard
No peaches and plums
Worse upstate
They got hit real bad
NY lost two-thirds
Conversation switched to
Great musicians
We lost Waylon Jennings
The Outlaw I said
Did you see him
No never
Me too
Got eleven albums
How 'bout Bowie and Prince
Yeah rough winter
Global warming nobody listens
My mom died some months ago
Cleaning out her stuff
In a drawer

Tickets to Music Inn
Bonnie Raitt was really great
Back in the day
Counting up the sale
On pad of paper
Ran my card
See you next year
Lord willing
Rock on brother
Hey, you OK man
Yeah just a little tired
Looks like you're
Near to cleaned out
It's been wicked busy
Remember that hot day
Hit the 90s in May
Nobody listens
Walmart forgot to water
Lost all their stock
Meant a run on us
Wouldn't have happened
If they paid them a living age
Pretty funny come to think
Serves them right

Farm Stand

Passing farm stand
Just up the road
Now early August
Sign finally hanging
For sweet Corn
Butter and Sugar
Tomatoes not yet ripe
Leave them in bag overnight
Young girl ring in her nose
Kids nowadays
Cautiously I asked
Where's the old lady
Passed last June
Remembered fondly
Small and frail
Bent with age
Toothless grin
Knew me well
Pleasant exchanges
Hot today ain't it
Sure is she said
In her pleasant way
Always there mostly alone
Slowly counting change
Worked her to death
I said with a laugh
The older woman
Perhaps her daughter
Answered from rocker
Try and get her
To take a day off

Great to see corn
Sweet and nice
On the grill last night
Really miss the old lady
A true friend of mine

Racine's no longer sells corn.

Lean Harvest

Mid-September with
Hot days and cool nights
No sign of frost
Still weeks away
Local farm stand
Racine's for fresh corn
Picked that day
Dinners on the deck
Last weekend she said
After Sunday end of the crop
Not like before
Usually lasts till mid-October
Month from now
Heat killed us though
Corn matured too early
Packing it in we're
Not coming back
That's it boss retiring
Had enough of farming
All work no pay
Tomatoes though
Up the hill
Least for now
Bucket of seconds
Feast for a week
Come winter
No point buying
Big Y just not the same
Ain't it a shame
Joys of summer
Getting scarce hereabouts

Last of Adams

From two to one
Once there were three
Closed yesterday
Turned in keys
Missing sweet Adams
View of Mt. Greylock
Our movie ever changing
Fifteen good years
Such lush summers
As of today just memories
Not far away
Sea of boxes in
Loft in North Adams
Close yet far
Yin and Yang
Pastoral there
Industrial here
Artist's loft in factory building
Where once
Children of the Mill
Labored dawn to dusk
King cotton haunts our home
Outer space
Sound of Hoosic River
Rushing by ebb and flow
Torrent in Spring
During mountain runoff
Then just a trickle
Summer drought
Like our life refocused
Rife with introspection
Time for reflection
So much to be done
Now all in one place

Homecoming

Holiday weekend
Memorial Day left Gloucester
Quarter of eleven
Last walk on the beach
Off-peak traffic
Beat the rush
Cruised actually
Hit the Pike
Stopped for lunch
In the Berkshires by 3:30 PM
Record time considering
BJ's for food
Then Adams to water
Home in our loft
Taking a break
She prepared
Tea with cheese and apples
Thanks but I needed
A stiff one
Stash depleted
End of the season
Before annual move
Next week
Just a splash of Meyer's Rum
Left from eggnog
Two years ago
In the fridge for a mixer
Yikes just prune juice
You know why
Always an issue
When on the road
What the heck

Glass with ice
Hefty pour
Splash of cripes prune juice
Talk about wicked
Joined her on couch
Shared snacks
Winding down our vacation
Perfect timing before the tourists
Took a swig
Smile on my face
Hey man not bad mate
Molasses of rum
Smooth and rich
Wedded to dark sugary fruit
Oddly matched perfect mélange
Medicinal cocktail
Gets you coming and going

View of Mt. Greylock in Adams.

Gloucester

Fisherman's Memorial, Gloucester.

Whipple House

On the town green
Land donated by Crane
Moved there 1927
Whipple House
Built in stages
Spacious and grand
John Winthrop the Younger
Son of governor
Massachusetts Bay Colony
Pious Pilgrims
Came in eleven ships
Hundreds God fearing
Many died off
Disease and starvation
Winter of 1630
First Nor'easter
Lost fingers and toes
Built house in stages
First half 1677
Then other side
Stout summer beams
Through and through
Shiver me timbers
Back lean-to later
Kitchen and slave quarters
Next to it a replica
Miserable thatched hut
One small room
Like most lived
The common man
Cramped and mean

Grim life in His Name
Witches and devils
Nestled in thatch
Tumbling down on
Rainy days of
Cats and dogs
Exploring the mansion
Furniture richly carved
Chests instead of closets
Seventeen spacious rooms
Next to hearths
Massive central chimney
Heat and cooking
Night and day
Local cottage industry
Intricate pillow lace
Inch by inch
Collars and cuffs
Fashionable pin money
Then first stocking mill
Plans stolen from England
Early industrial espionage
Brought jobs and people
Mill shut down
No new housing
Town a time capsule
Frozen like Salem
Newburyport to Nantucket
Colonial archaeology
Hard living from
Ship building and farming

Marsh and salt hay
Rural and poor
Before clam shacks
Best in the world
Priced like gold
Bumper to bumper
On a summer day
Bogged down in Essex
For early settlers
Herbs by the kitchen
Sprigs of this and that
Fer what ails ye
Potent potions
Heaven or hell
Day in the stocks
Neighbors to gawk
Repent ye sinners
Lord have mercy
On your soul

On the Beach

Rugged rocky coast
Giant boulders of craggy granite
Buttresses against giant waves
Raging storms on the beach
Hold on tight closing ranks
Bracing for deluge
Watching it come from out at sea
Now rolling near to shore
Cresting white wall of water
Crashing over linked mass
Breaking the line
Some washed away
Ferocious riptide
Those remaining regrouped
Stand fast mates
The rally cry
Up and down the line
Here comes another
Hearty defenders
Defying nature's rage
Gloucester's elders
Old salts with tales to tell
Storms remembered
Long ago swept away
Brave generations
Of lost souls

Saga of Howard Blackburn

Out of Gloucester
Aboard sleek schooner
Grace L. Fears
From the mother ship
Two men in a dory
Howard Blackburn (1859-1932)
To fish all day
Cod and halibut
Lost in snow squall
Off Newfoundland
Thomas Welch (1857-1883)
Died the second day
Kept bailing
Lost his mittens
Fingers frozen
Cupped around oars
Kept rowing
Flesh falling off
Four days on
Reached land
Night in a shack
Back in the dory
Farmer's wife
Mrs. Lishman
Snipped off fingers
With her scissors
Half of each thumb
Five toes amputated
Two from left three right
Heel of one foot
Hobbled home

Cheating Davy Jones
Hero's welcome
Opened tobacco store
Locals raised $500
Paid back more
Than three times over
Donated $50,000 to charities
A fortune for the time
Met and married tiny
Theresa Lally (1863-1931)
They lost their son
Negligent nurse
Dose of cough medicine
Six weeks old
Built a saloon
Made a fortune
Folks swarmed in
Watched him pick up tips
A sight to see
What with no fingers
Went back to sea
Over and over
25-foot sloop
Great Republic
Solo to Portugal
Other voyages
Sold it in Florida
Bought a rowboat
Boca Raton to Jacksonville
Quit half way
Took steamer home

Then dory America
Gloucester to France
Such was the plan
Month of storms
Turned back
That was it
Spinning tales
Off the Grand Banks
When God was cod

Dory, Rockport Harbor, like the one Blackburn used.

Breakwater

The Flynns hearty Irish lads
Grandfather's family
Settled in Canada
Quarrymen made their way to
New Hampshire
The Granite State
Where James was born
Moved to Rockport
Worked the stone
Alongside Finns
Brawny men
Leaving vast pits
Now filled with water
Fed by springs
Risky swimming
Bottomless deep
Looking out from
Tip of Rockport's
Bearskin Neck
The vast breakwater
My family
Labored to create
Bulwark against
Breaking waves
Fierce winter storms
Sheltering tranquil Sandy Bay
Manet in Latin for granite
Means it endures

Note in a Bottle

Washed up on a beach
Sands of time and tide
Note in a bottle
Marooned by desolate space
Scribbled message
To an unknown reader
Neither friend nor family
Perfect stranger
Lonely ranger
Words as silver bullets
Piercing the void
Now or when
Decades hence
Perhaps centuries
You are curious
What was back then
Probing the motive
Book sitting on a shelf
Library anywhere
Possibly a yard sale
Or plucked from the trash
Stumbled upon
Sublime serendipity
These words so intense
Surviving my mortality
Connecting now to you
Who I never knew
But loved dearly
Object of this verse
However muddled
Utterly perverse

Strange and terse
Reduced to an essence
Ashes and dust
Burnt offering
Tossed in the wind

Lighthouse Beach, Annisquam.

Time and Tide

Rockport
Where Nugent ancestors
Founded vast clan
Beaver Dam Farm
Irish lads with gift of gab
Colorful blarney
Town split from Gloucester
1840 the archivist said
Helping with research
Scant evidence
Bright Monday morning
Quiet for shops
Bearskin Neck
Sentimental art
Sagas of the sea
Depicted as kitsch
Not epic drama
Of Winslow Homer
Toilers of the deep
Now mostly lobster men
The ocean depleted overfished
Global warming
No more mussels clinging to rocks
Now farm raised Prince Edward Island
Water like glass
No breeze clear reflection
Motif Number One
Gawked at destination
Calendar pictures
Picturesque signifier
An actual lobster boat

Going about its business
Me clicking away
Like every rube
While my blood
Runs red in
Tranquil Sandy Bay

A sandpiper darts in and out of the waves.

Clambake on Lighthouse Beach

Relatively new to
Annisquam 1950s
Quiet Water in Algonquin
Upscale summers
Yacht Club picnic
Indian style clambake
Light House Beach
Started that morning
Roaring fire stones added
Splitting with heat
Seaweed harvested
Piled on in thick layers
Then lobsters
Mesh sacks of steamers
Corn and potatoes
More seaweed
Covered with wet sand
Packed down
Forming a mound
Kiln actually
Simmered till dusk
Sand brushed off
Goodies dug out
Served with butter
Feast by the shore
High tide of memory

Twin Lights

Late May in Gloucester
Familiar turf
Researching ancestors
Libraries and museums
Little or nothing
On Nugents of Rockport
Widening the net
Digging deeper
From the deck
Our room with a view
Twin Lights
Former beacons
In fog and storms
Keeping vessels
From its rocks
Sheltering cove
With surfers one day
Bathers the next
First rays pre-summer
Returning late August
Gloucester Writers Center
Meeting literary elite
Tales of Olson yet another
Charles oracle of briny deep
Where sailors sleep

Cape Cod

Ocean Edge. Photo by Astrid Hiemer.

Spring Awakening

Through snow and sleet
Narrow streets still asleep
Not a soul in sight
Nights in Provincetown
Still shuttered
No hint of summer's mayhem
Fishing village
Transformed to Sodom
For some who come
Seeking sin and pleasure
Enjoying the weather
Early April hunkered down
Ocean strolls brisk on the beach
Hint of what was
When artists first came
Some from Paris
Americans abroad
Gay and bohemian
During WWI
Back home from over there
Dread of Flanders Field
Where dead piled up
Starving pioneers
Saving money for paints
They lived on fish
Cheap on the dock
Waded for clams
Oysters by the bucket
Fisherman's stew
Hearty kale and
Linguica for tasty

Portuguese soup
Tip of Cape Cod
Last stop to Europe
From here to there
Daily reflections
Time and tide
Waiting for Lefty
Where no news is good news
Riding out the horror
Digging tunnels
Castles in the sand

Provincetown Dunes.

Long Point

Thrusting into the Atlantic
Tip of Cape Cod
Furthest point east land's end
Hook forming Provincetown harbor
Fishing town where artists walk
Its narrow streets
Long Point a former gallery
Spacious top floor
Old schoolhouse
Once studio of Leo Manso
Invited friends to share the rent
On site long ago
When hanging a show
Artists gathered Robert Motherwell
So casual in shorts
Discussing work with Tony Vevers
Artist Tabitha's handsome father
In vintage photo Sideo Fromboluti
Adjusting glasses pushed back
Wife Nora Speyer looking on
Bob chatting with an O'Donnell sister
She ran the gallery while
Ellen of Provincetown Art Association
Helped with basic research
Dissertation on Karl Knaths
Never happened
Life got in the way
So typical in the arts
Insights of our DNA
Conjuring thoughts
Of long ago at the Point

Rude Intruder

Along the shore
Week on Cape Cod
Glorious day by the sea
Bright sunny sublime
More August than October
Walking the water's edge
Busy sandpipers dawn to dusk
Working the waves
Such incredible speed
Constant pecking for food
Seagulls plopped on the sand
Blobs of feathers at rest
The young mottled but grown
Soaring above playing on the wind
Gliding more for sport
Windsurfers riding puffy gusts
Paused to sit on plastic chair
Now abandoned private beach
Your offensive chain link fence
Defining an absurd claim
Marring my view
Pristine nature defiled
By your disgusting arrogance
Cottages closed off-season
You not there to shoo me away
Reveling in righteous hubris
Defiantly sat gazing at my ocean
Diamonds of light flashing on waves
Sand sea and sky
The very tides belonged to me
I am nature itself
Now and forever
From sea to shining sea

Beach Detritus

Soft rain mid-October
First morning
Week on the Cape
Walking the beach
Tourists long gone
End of frenzy
Alone with the sea
Along the tide line
Mix of weeds
Scrabbled detritus
First one then another
Lots of them
Genocide of horseshoe crabs
Ancient warriors of the deep
Old as dinosaurs
Odd creatures
Underwater armor
Crawling on the bottom
That single lance
Unicorns it seems
Spears for predators
Washed up in droves
A mass killing
Mixed in with snails
Covered with barnacles
Clumped in clusters
Wondered what ailed them
Taking snapshots
Documenting beach stroll
Considering the slaughter
Cruelty of nature
Likely our fault

Beach littered with dead horseshoe crabs. Photo by Astrid Hiemer.

Stowe, Vermont

Frosted pines.

Stowe Birds

Frost on the windows
Our cabin in Stowe
Looking out on
Fresh tracks in new snow
Cross-country skier
Small dog leaping behind
Short legs churning
Shaking off slumber
Quiet nights
Like that Miles album
Reading his bio sheeet mofo
About Bird, Diz and Trane
Shooting scag what a drag
Strange fruit for The Holidays
What hipsters do in the woods
Digging bop for the Holidays
Birth of the Cool for kid in the crib
Catching up on memories
Text speaking jive
His raspy voice
Like being there
Belly up to the bar
Side by side at Paul's Mall
Between sets long ago
Silent Nights broken when he said
Give the ofay mofo a drink
Yeah baby here's to you
For this holidays on ice
Laying back in the woods
With a head full of bop

While fay's slide by
On slick slopes
See and ski

Top of Mt. Mansfield in Stowe.

Tourist Trapp

Cold, clean and crisp
Bright sunny day
Winter wonderland
Sunday drive in Vermont
Famous Trapp Family Lodge
Alpine kitsch sprawling and corporate
Not exactly Edelweiss
Hardly Sound of Music
More like clinging cash register
Where the rich play
Fun on the slopes with
Visa, MasterCard and American Express
Pleasures of gaudy excess
Viewing the formal dining room
Severe and austere
Upscale schnitzel
Servers in dirndls with frosty smiles
Downhill to Bierhalle for lunch
She loved the ginger ale
Best ever Astrid said
For me instead
Ale but no ginger
Weak and too pale
Frozen a watery winter brew
One of several
Touted as seasonal quaff
Wheat or chaff
Then a shop full of crap
Souvenirs of Trapp
Hoodies and trinkets
Coasters and key rings

Reminders of refugees
Band on the run
Making it big
In corporate tourism

Trapp Family Lodge.

Peak Experience

Twist and turn along 108
Stowe's Mountain Road
Past motels, resorts, restaurants
Base of Mt. Mansfield
Elevation 4,395 feet
Looking up at trails
Broad swaths swaggering
Blazed through pines
Spectacular snow sculptures
Frosted op art patterns
Brilliant clear blue sky
Blazing northern light
In the gondola's endless ascent
Swing and sway
Way above skiers
Criss-crossing below
How ironic compared to
Porto just a month ago
November more like summer
Above the Douro River
Similar but different
Conflated impressions
Slowing to a halt we
Exited to arctic blast
Colder than a witch's tit
Geared up against elements
With helmets and goggles
Some with face masks
Preparing their runs
Snowboarders strapping in
Surfing on snow
Cresting on frozen tsunami

Midweek not much traffic
No lines for the lift
Just before Christmas
Slow day on the slopes
Making our way to the crest
Up against the rope
Magnificent treacherous view
Fearing for my life
She called me back
Asking why did you do that
For the thrill I said
What mountains are for
Looking down and about
I could see for miles
And miles and miles
Like clear still morning
After acid trip at Benno's
Night of Moosh Magique
Dancing in the hearth
Kaleidoscope of memory
Way off yonder
Imposing Mt. Washington
Simply sublime
Highlight of our time
In frozen chosen
Wacko snowbirds
Craggy lovers
Slip sliding along
Chilled to the bone
Flew the wrong way
Who knew it would be
So deliciously divine

Udder Madness

Green Mountain state
Verdant Vermont
Land of milk and honey
More cows than people
What to do with all that dairy
Make lots of moolah
Ben and Jerry's ice cream
Cherry Garcia
Now gone global
Not locally sourced
Like back in the day
Visiting Cabot Cheese
Small samples spiked
On toothpicks
Every kind of cheddar
From a thousand farms
Over hill and dale
Exploring local microbrews
Quaffing hard cider
From all them apples
Wallowing in pastures
Thick with shit that
Flavors the grass
Sweetens the cream
Udder madness
Rolling down hills
Running in rivers
Bright with trout
Tooling about
Four-wheel drive
Slip and slide

Far from home
But not alone
Cloudy gray days
Steady drizzle
Slush on windshield
While cattle munch hay
We come to play
Celebrating the holiday

In the summer the bus sells ice cream.

Stowe Away

Sensible seniors
Our friends and neighbors
Snowbirds all
Fly South for winter
Florida, Mexico
Cruises in the Caribbean
Hardy souls stay home
Hunker by the hearth
If they have one
Read and work on projects
Contrarians like us
Counter intuitive
Headed north for
A week in Stowe
Life in a cabin
Warm and cozy
Setting up housekeeping
Not hitting the slopes
Charlie don't surf but
Loves the smell of morning
Fresh snow it seems
Brushed off the car
Then out and about
Shelburne Museum
Drive to Burlington
Trapp Family Lodge
More fun at Ben and Jerry's
In liberal Vermont
Bernieland of upscale socialism
Dinners at fun places
Or pretentious ones

Where only prices
Are truly impressive
Days of whine and roses
Sleep perchance to dream
Of Sugar Plum Fairies
A winter interlude
Both cure and cause
Of cabin fever

Backyard grill of our cottage in Stowe.

Stowe Storm

Started slow in the AM
Wipeout by noon
Inch by inch all day
Great for the slopes
Week before Christmas
When Stowe gets slammed
Hunkered down
Laptop, books and Netflix
Kindah cabin feverish
Last day away
Moonlight in Vermont
Tea and snacks snowbound
No fancy dinner tonight
Out on Mountain Road
With so many options
Pensioners on holiday
Snap happy snuggled bunnies
Having the time of our lives
Iconic winter wonderland
Quaint New England village
Dressed for the Holidays
Bright light of twinkling cheer
Has its ambivalence
Listening now to Astrid
Cracking pistachio nuts
Hardly chestnuts by a roaring fire
Here today but gone tomorrow
Remembering spectacular yesterday
On magnificent Mt. Mansfield
Such towering wonder
Trees painted white

Nature's canvas a luminist landscape
Our time so sublime
Slipping into quotidian
Said the comedian
Such fools we mortals be
Take two he said
With sardonic mirth
One makes you tall the other small
Better red than dead
On the whole better in Philadelphia
If you catch my snow drift
Plowing through metaphors
Before and after

Snow falling behind our Stowe cabin.

Tom Cruises Venice.

Depth in Venice

On the road to and fro
Some years ago
Deep in the heart of Texas
Houston's de Menil
Its magnificent Rothko Chapel
Round room of fourteen paintings
Dark and spiritual deep as sleep
Prayer and introspection
Bibles and Korans
Strewn about
Space to meditate
Hushed whispers
Reached for my phone
Called Mark in Boston
Sharing the experience
Later a staggering bill
For roaming charges
Again last night
Lagoon in Venice
Lido actually a plebian beach
No tourists not even Swiss
Or great Danes with gloomy souls
Row of worker shacks
Where locals bathe and frolic
Spectacular blue sky
Diamonds glistening on water
Boisterous boys sons of gondoliers
Many Tadzios cavorting about
Frisky games in bikini trunks
Of every possible bright color
So wonderful to be there

Reveling in Mann
His evocative novella
Yet again on my phone
Compelling impulse
To call Mark
Screw the cost
Sharing the sublime but
Messed up mishegoss
Friggin' loss as I awoke
Soft gray light of
Winter in the Berkshires
Sublime home with
No roaming charges
For my mortal coil

The Grand Canal, Venice.

Jesus in the Heartland.

Bleeding Kansas

Namby Pamby
This and That
Here and There
So it goes
Back and forth
Day to day
Hither and yawn
More or less
Who's to say
One way or other
Works and Days
According to Hesiod
Them friggin' Greeks
So old school
Endless toil our
Mortal coil
Laboring in vineyards
Of the Lord
Such sweet wine
Man oh shoveits
Soaked in bread
Body and blood
Loaves and fishes
Feeding multitudes
Perfect strangers
As if anyone really
Is strange or perfect
Odd as it seems
Blind faith
Crop of Cream
Out there in Kansas

Land of wheat
Roadside crosses
Jeepin jiminy
Like Spartacus
Near porn shops
Farmer in the dell
Fast track to hell
Along highways
To heaven
Staff of life
In heartless land
Where not much matters

Blind Faith.

New York

Statue of Liberty.

Naked City

Feeling small the immensity of it all
New York City East Side, West Side
All around the town
People as ants scurrying about
Museums and theatre swaths of art
Overwhelmingly spiraling Guggenheim
Ramped up with contemporary China
Social sculpture both
Powerful and poignant
Spin cycles stunned at every turn
Stops to pee at every level
Wright was thoughtful
Tiny closets for creature comforts
Beasts that we are
TKTS in Times Square
Light traffic Tuesday and Halloween
Ghouls and action heroes
Macabre traffic glides by
Pretty girls with painted faces
Such a fun night
Everyone as someone else
Like Patti LuPone with a limp
Helena Rubinstein in War Paint
Christine Ebersole as Elizabeth Arden
Magnificent divas duking it out
Intermission chat with
John Douglas Thompson between shows
Bringing Carousel to Broadway
His first musical a non-singing role
Ending a day of such play
Nightcap at National Arts Club

Venerable Tiffany lounge
Enjoying revelers in costumes
Remnants of a celebration
Then up to 7C how suite it is
In city that never sleeps

Times Square.

Hot Town

Such a scorcher
Sidewalks melting
Lower East Side
303 East 11th Street
Electricity turned off
No AC food spoiled
Candles at night
Gas though
Fairly cheap
Hot water and coffee
Bathtub in the kitchen
Between gallery gigs
Living on the dole
Employed come fall
Kids gone wild
Hydrants opened
Playing with water
Keeping cool
Raising hell
Tin can open both ends
Jump out of nowhere
Quick squat
Gusher redirected
Neat trick
Powerful blast
Aimed at open windows
Of passing cars
Howls of laughter
Driver drenched
One got out chased Loco
Caught up broke his leg

Hobbled about
Rest of summer
Hard lesson learned
Grew up deranged
Urban jungle where
Only the strong survive

Hockney in Chelsea.

California

Golden Gate Bridge.

Summer of Love

Fifty years later
Summer of Love
Perhaps really wasn't
Media concoction
Flower power
Teenyboppers
Hitching to San Francisco
Acid tests
Those classic bands
Playing for free
Golden Gate Park
Owsley Sunshine
Wiggy man
Far ffffen out
They gasped
Kaleidoscope
Visions splashing
Over inner space
Mandala movies
Gazing at lava lamps
Now not so groovy
No illusions
Summer of Hate
Klan rallies
Open carry weapons
Torchlight parades
Blue and Gray
Statues toppled
Robert E. Lee
Stonewall Jackson
Icons of racism

The Gallant South
Strange Fruit
Celebrating Jim Crow
Making America Great
Alt-Right racists
Zero tolerance for
Neo-Nazis
No two sides
One Nation Indivisible
Now and forever

Signed, Seals, Delivered.

The Rock

The Rock
Island of the Pelicans
Alcatraz
Blight on San Francisco Bay
Grim reminder
Brutal inhumanity
Stir-crazy
Federal pen 1934 to 1963
Harbor cruise
Brisk breeze
Numbing water
Swift currents
Notorious inmates
Al Capone to Machine Gun Kelly
Boston mobster Whitey Bulger
Robert Franklin Stroud
AKA Birdman of Alcatraz
Worst of the worst
14 escape attempts
By 36 prisoners
Captured, killed or drowned
Maybe four made it
Never found
Terrible place
Cruel and unusual
60 guards and families
For 250 prisoners
Crumbling and costly
Feds opened Leavenworth
Not much better
Tough nut to crack

Native Americans
Reclaimed the island
19 months in 1969
Wounded Knee by the sea
Now tourist trap
Gape and gawk
Where gulls squawk
Chip off the old cell block
Film noir in vivid colors

The Rock, Alcatraz Island, San Francisco Bay.

Nature Boy

Not just an American
I am America
It's every bit of me
Mountains and sea
Mother Earth
Part and parcel
The very essence
Forests once primeval
Pure and pristine
Before Europeans came
Hopes and dreams
Including my ancestors
Irish and Sicilian
More benign than most
Slaughtered no Natives
Didn't own slaves
First generations
Scratched the earth
Tilled hardscrabble soil
In rocky Rockport
Sold fruit in Brooklyn
Spawning me it seems
Owner of this earth
Surveying all I see
Mountains and prairies
Feasting on bounty of oceans
Visiting National Parks
At least for now
Set aside for all of us
Bulwarks against greed
Towering trees
Deep gorges in the earth

Polluted lakes and rivers
Running through them
Once leaping trout and salmon
Deer, bears and antelope
Tsunamis of buffalo
Packs of wolves
Culling the herds
All mine this land
In the traditions of
Walt Whitman and Woody Guthrie
Their sanguine poetry
Traveling troubadours
Richly wrought verse
During war and depression
Just rephrasing and updating
Lest they be lost
Shut down like filibusters
Informed verbal protestors
Against defilers of
Our precious land and heritage
What's left of global dignity
Assaulted by ignorance and greed
Prejudice and intolerance
Still proud to be an American
Though bashed and battered
Sullied and assaulted
All through the nightmare
Our flag still stands
This land is your land
This land is my land
Don't tread on me

Into the Woods

Heat wave
Leaving San Francisco
Over Golden Gate Bridge
Past Sausalito by the Bay
Mountain goat descent
Twisting and turning
Deep into a gorge
Inaccessible for logging
So spared the axe
Stand of ancient redwoods
Preserved for the people
Magnificent Muir Woods
Impossible to park
We got lucky
Following planked path
Options for visits
Short, medium, and long
Test of stamina
Immediate coolness
Fragrant scented air
Every breath you take
Rich vegetation
Immense trees
Enormous girth
Flora and fauna
Deep in the forest
Exotic reflections
Thousands of years
Standing so tall
Towering above
Filtered sky

Dappled mosaic light
Staggering nature
Spiritual sublime
Signifiers of time
Precious heritage
For all Americans
Commonality of wonder
Reminder of what was
Before New World
Decimated primeval one
Murmuring pines and hemlock
Tree to bounding sea

A cluster of redwoods.

Signed Seals Delivered

Harbor cruise
Under Golden Gate Bridge
Loop around Alcatraz
Choppy water
Cold swift currents
San Francisco Bay
Back to Pier 39
Fisherman's Wharf
Crammed with tourists
Past docks
Massed with sea lions
Gawking tourists
Jammed together
Basking in sun
Flipper to flipper
Slipping off
Now and then
Plunging deep
Graceful and sleek
Feeding on fish
Such a charmed life
Big old bulls
Bellow their turf
Newborn seals
Swim from day one
Taking it easy
These sleek sea creatures
Gentle and breezy
California Dreaming
On a dock of the bay

Sea Span

Brisk headwind
Choppy in the Bay
Whitecaps on water
Salt in my face
Lurching about
Holding on tight
Near the prow
Windsurfers zooming
To leeward
Shrouded in fog
Mighty span
Over under and around
Golden Gate Bridge
Marvel of engineering
Back then said
Couldn't be done
Stretching across
Shore-to-shore
Sailing ever closer
Snapping away
The grid above us
Patterns of girders
Symphony of waves
Engines as tympani
Gulls taking solos
Wagnerian opera
Under then around
Turning back The Rock
Circling grim Alcatraz
Where tourists scramble
Docking at the pier
Sea lions basking

Sonoma

From the balcony
The square below
Statue under wraps
Guarded last night
Until dawn
Against rowdy revelers
This sweet town
About 10,000 souls
Winemakers and pensioners
Tipsy tourists
Staggering from tasting rooms
Some thirty or so
Within walking distance
Where once were
Groceries and hardware stores
Now gentrified
Daze of wine and roses
Tasted some 24 yesterday
Mostly spat
Except for high-end ones
Forty bucks on up
Exotic vintages of
Just a hundred cases
Me who never drinks
Before supper
Never friggin Chardonnay
Too buttery and oaked up
Tried the new ones
Fermented in steel
Fresh and cleaner
Evenings a half bottle

Mostly French
Set down a few years
Vineyards far as the eye can see
Here to Napa Valley
Unveiling this afternoon
Celebrating General Vallejo
Founder of Sonoma
Last mission of Franciscans
Bringing Jesus to California
Swiss Hotel where I scribble this
1850s adobe home
Of esteemed general's brother
Later expanded
Cozy and charming
Just five rooms
Local legends
We never knew
Before being there

Well-tended vineyards.

Matriarch with great-grand son, Senegal. Photo by Astrid Hiemer.

Gorée Island

That day on the ferry
Eight years ago
In Senegal
Newly-elected
President Obama
A time of Hope
Setting off from Dakar
Soft breeze
Bound for Gorée Island
Ever closer
Looming fortress
Solemn walk
Via Dolorosa
Stations to cross
Trail of tears
Endless processions
Sting of the lash
Streets now lined
With merchants
Tourist trinkets
With measured steps
Approaching
Maison des Esclaves
Colonial mansion
Master's quarters
A rustic museum
Memorabilia evoking
Hell of its
Grim rooms below
Holding cells
Either side of

Narrow corridor
At its end
Radiant with light
Door of no return
Stepping up
Looking out
Rocky shore
Ocean beyond
First steps
Down a ramp
Boarding ships
Middle Passage
From which none
Returned
Barack and Michelle
Stood in that door
A black woman
In our group
Wept for days
Another at the beach
Plunged into the waves
Holding a photo
Of her grandmother
I have returned for her
She shared with me
Feeling the depth of
America's shame
Retreating back to
What America was
Before a black president
Gave us Hope

Middle Passage

That winter in Senegal
Different drummers
Rough trip
Going native with Pip
No amenities
Dead broke
Dusty roads
Bumpy busses
Tough hotel
Bread for breakfast
Lunch of stinky fish
Over smelly rice
Beautiful beaches
Soccer and dancers
Hello my brother
Endless hustle
Throngs of kids
Bare feet begging change
Cattle wandering streets
Watched from rooftop
Obama had just won
World changed
So it seemed
Poignant to be there
Visiting Gorée Island
Slaves shipped in chains
Hopes for difference
Later generation
Born in the USA
Back at the source

The Middle Passage
How much has changed

A statue, Gorée Island, Senegal.

Portugal

Bridges in Porto.

Spanning Lisboa

Day one in Lisboa
A short nap then
Off to the bus
Dazed and crazed
Lost then found
Down the hill with Brad
On and off that afternoon
Lunch al fresco
Cod of course
Curse God and die
Tippling port
As is his want
Then back on top
Whirling round and about
Could it be says me
Ponte 25 de Abril
Suspension bridge
That iconic bright orange
Spanning Tagus River
Acid flashbacks
My heart in San Francisco
Catapulted to June
Our summer of love
Iconic Golden Gate Bridge
But with Rio Jesus on top
How oddly Portuguese
Vast arms outstretched
Embracing the faithful
Launched as Salazar Bridge
August 6, 1966
Renamed for bloodless

Carnation Revolution
Commemorating
Ouster of dictator
Now free since 1974
Indeed a site to see

Excursion boats in Porto.

City of Bridges

TAP wine tour
Several days from
Dawn to dusk
On and off the bus
Visiting quintas
Five wines at a time
Sip and spit
Elegant dining
Michelin chefs
Endless variations
Locally sourced
Appropriate pairings
A taste of Portugal
Exhausting orgy of flavors
Ending in Porto
Daze of wine and roses
Friday on my own
Exploring the city
Its daunting hills
Gondola down to
Douro River
Late November
More like August
Chance encounter
Joined Phil and Maria
Prow of the boat
Tour of the river
Exploring City of Bridges
Cruising under spans
Gliding past centuries
Dense packed banks

Caves and warehouses
Shipping fortified wines
Thriving industry
When the sun never set
That fine day
Bathed by memory

Cable Car over Douro River.

Porto in a Storm

What started in Lisboa
Resumed in Porto
Madcap pursuit of Poe's
Cask of Amontillado
Spelunking deep cave
Kerplunking nine circles
Hell-bound hipsters
Brad as my Virgil
Along the Douro River
Exquisite rare vintages
A 1964 white port
Exploding in my mouth
A billiards sensation
Bank shots careening
Cheeks to tongue
Smashing up into
Pulsating palate
Raucous aftershocks
Sensation of a lifetime
Perhaps never duplicated
Daunting hefty price
Rare fortified wine
Tested by time
Such sweet thunder
Compare and contrast
Class after glass
Such lessons learned
That sublime afternoon
Down the rabbit hole
Lonely oenophiles
So far from home

Seduced by a
Bacchic haze
Now mythic days
Raising the bar
Beneath a bridge too far
Down by the Douro
Me and Julio

Rome

Whom the gods love die young.

March Madness

Et Tu!
Three and two
The big one due
Me and Julio
Down by the Forum
Orange Julius
Let it bleed
Citizen soldier
Who would be emperor
Hail Caesar
Man of the people
Loved by plebeians
Master of spectacle
Panem et circenses
Sweet Republic
Slain by ambition
Greed for power
Thirst of adulation
Down for the count
Awash bathed in
His own blood
Imperial purple
Now foul incarnadined
Come let me hug thee
Valiant warrior
Veni, Vidi, Vici
You're so vain
This song is about you
Soft embrace
Thrust not trust
Proud Brutus

Friend now foe
Unkindest cut
Ashes to ashes
Blowing in the wind
Of infamy
Fate of tyrants
Intoxicated by
Sweet smell of
Their own shit

Ancient Bath England from Roman times.

Juvenal's Satires

Belly of the beast
Sloshing about
Decaying muck
Rot of Empire
Putrid flesh
Mordant observer
Sharp eye
Vicious tongue
Sixteen Satires
Vivid commentary
Comical compilation
All the phobes
Condensed and vile
Misanthropic
Homophobic
Xenophobic
Particularly Greeks
Egyptians reviled
Where he was banished
Under terrible Domitian
Savage to patrician women
Decimus Junius Juvenalis
Petty bourgeois rentier
Reduced in station
Inspired creation
Rude and bitter
Dependent on patrons
Whom he reviled
Known as Juvenal
May have been
Born 55–60 AD

Perhaps died in 127

Little is known

The work survives

Stunning images

Sweating in a toga

Carnage of the games

Lawyer in chiffon

Succinct phrases

Bread and circus

Who will guard the guards themselves

The itch for writing

Bronze statue of Sejanus

Former favorite

Slaughtered by

Decadent Tiberius

Melted down for

Chamber pots

Society matron

Lathering herself

Rare emollients

Costly cosmetics

Resulting in

Is that a face, or an ulcer

The lady who

Has her slave flogged

For a misplaced curl

The arriviste

A rich Greek

Who dines alone

On a roasted boar

Brawls in brothels

Couples who cheat
Boys or gladiators
Eunuchs preferred
Pumiced cheeks
Delicious diversion
Guilty pleasure
Not for the squeamish
Mirror held up
Reflecting our image
Millennials amuck
Ambitious greed
Self-absorbed
Decadent luxuries
Hooking up
Lapsing into
Ninth circle
Our hell as Earth
Not just other people
Read him and weep
Our pristine universe
Rape so perverse

Augustus

In front of bathroom mirror
After a shower gazing intently
From all sides reflecting on
What greatly resembles
Given my Sicilian heritage
Regal bearing of a Roman Emperor
Augustus perhaps
At the very least
A Senator perhaps Cicero
Ceterum censeo Carthaginem esse delendam
I would orate in the Forum
Before gathered Plebeians
Like Commodus
I might entertain them
Fighting as a Gladiator
Always the winner
Feeling rather imperial
With arrogant swagger
Stood naked before Astrid
Striking an Augustan pose
A living god loved by Jupiter
Hail Caesar they proclaimed
Grand and commanding
Espoused my theory
What do you think
Amused she replied
Not really with a smirk
They had bigger noses

Domus Aurea

Roman Emperors
Intimidate and rule
Through spectacle
Erecting walls
Buildings palaces
Rampant paranoia
Keeping out barbarians
Hadrian's feared Scots
Decadent palaces
Lavish entertainment
Domus Aurea
Nero's Golden House
Heart of Rome
Some 200 acres
After great fire 64 AD
300-room palace
Marble and gold
Mosaic and fresco
Man-made lake
Public parks fragrant gardens
Feasts with favorites
Forty years after Nero's suicide
Palace abandoned
An embarrassment
Monument to oppression
Rooms filled in
Lake drained
Over it built
Flavian Amphitheatre
Nero's 120-foot bronze Colossus
Dragged there by elephants

Renamed Coliseum
Where gladiators saluted
Nos morituri te salutamus
Amusing the masses
Choking in blood

Three Graces.

Trivia

All roads lead to Rome
Scotland to Syria
Population of 55 million
Well-paved network
Where three converged
From the Latin Tri Via
Notes posted
For fellow travelers
Morphed today as trivia
Flood of useless information
Bits and pieces our daytime TV
Vulgarian talk shows
Gossip as insights
Concocting recipes
Pseudo celebrities
Ersatz pundits on
Dr. Shill or Ellen dancing
Author tours for
Books you'll never read
Latest movie stars
Talk radio's blithering blather
CNN without end
All news all day
Yak, yak, yak
Trash rehashed
Stupid game shows
Family Fools or
Nirvana turning letters
Jeopardy questions
Test our intelligence
Travesty of facts and figures

Trump's tweets
Even his fake news
Began at the crossroads
From pillar to post

The good life depicted on a Roman sarcophagus.

Fayum Portraits

Cleopatra last of the Ptolemys
Gave Caesar a son
Heir to an Empire
More Greek than Egyptian
Battle of Actium with Marc Antony
2 September 31 BC
Fleet sunk by Octavian
Romans seduced by Osiris
Exotic rituals Cult of Isis
Added to Pantheon
Colonists were buried
In the Egyptian tradition
Not cremated but mummified
Their portraits added
In the Roman manner
Honoring filial piety
Stunning images
Facile encaustic
Masterful rendering
Facing eternity
Just as they were
Jeweled matron
Swarthy merchant
Tender child
Gazing back at us
Depicting miscegenation
That genetic confluence
So reviled by Juvenal who
Abhorred foreigners
Exiled on the Nile
Ironically inferior even

To lowly Greeks
Impoverished patrician
Longing for Rome

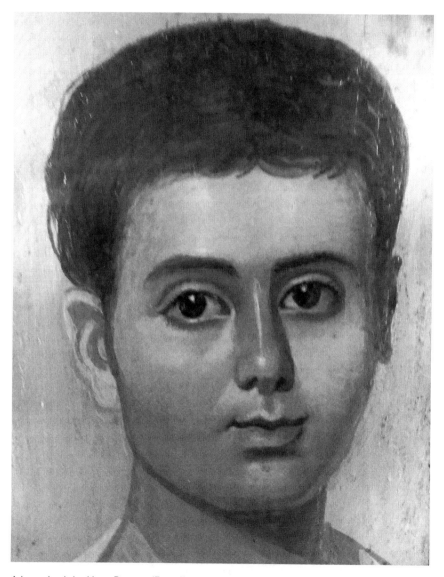

A boy depicted in a Roman/Egyptian mummy mask.

Pea-Brained Emperor

Utterly absurd
Ridiculous in fact
Heroic bronze statue
Roman Emperor
Trebonianus Gallus
With son Gaius Vibius Volusianus
Co-ruled AD 251 to 253
Both slaughtered
Frenzied mutiny
Brutally mutilated
Once most powerful
Men on earth
Difficult times
Surging barbarians
Fragile frontiers
Constant wars
Plots intrigues
Callow cabals
Reigned long enough
To commission
Buck-naked portrait
Who was he kidding
Hail Caesar
Laughing stock
Emperor unclothed
Citizens snickered
Ersatz stud
Vainglorious pose
Mens sana in corpore sano
De facto insana caputa
Tiny head teetering on

Barrel-chested torso
Like puffed up Rome
Bloated with greed
Ripe for slaughter
Delusions of glory
Lewdly ludicrous
That silly donkey
Who would be king

The Emperor Nude.

Commodus the Gladiator Emperor

Tipping point
When and why
Empires decline and fall
Perhaps Commodus (161-192 AD)
Twelve-year reign of terror
Ending in assassination
Son of Marcus Aurelius (121-180 AD)
Last of Five Good Emperors
Philosopher King
Platonic ideal like Alexander
Tutored by Aristotle
His Meditations still read
Commander on the Rhine
Holding the line
Empire of 55 million
He slept in tents not palaces
Toughened his son
To no avail
His corrupt heir
Made peace with tribes
Indifferent to detail
Devoted to pleasure
Corruption prevailed
Delegated power
Played and betrayed
Sister Lucilla seducing senators
She plotted his death
Killed her instead
Chaos reigned
Cleander blamed
Plague and famine

City burned
Vowed to rebuild
In his name proclaimed
Fourteen days of games
Fifty thousand shouted his name
In the arena as gladiator
Killed weakened opponents
Guise of Hercules
Anointed by Jupiter
Dismantled senate
Renamed Rome
Colonia Lucia Annia Commodiana
Months dedicated to him
No end of excess
Orders to kill enemies
Real and imagined
Murdered by Narcissus
Gladiator and trainer
Civil War then
Year of Five Emperors
Ever more divided
The end more whimper than bang
476 AD when unopposed
Child Emperor deposed
Barbarian Odovacar walked in
Refusing the purple
Empire split but in the East
Byzantium prevailed until 1453
When defeated Constantinople
Renamed as Islam's Istanbul
Two and a half centuries

After Commodus
When things fell apart
Like us perhaps
How near the end

Commodus as Hercules.

Slice of Life

Sic transit gloria mundi
Purest white marble
Galvanic classical beauty
Adonis his perfect features
Severed in the Met
Fragment of glory
All that remains
Toppled smashed to pieces
Rudely assaulted
Whom the gods loved
Perished still young
Agile yet fragile
Peak of perfection
Not suffering sorrows of age
No ruts or wrinkles
Marring alabaster perfection
Remarkably radiant
Paradigm of Platonic ideals
Fraternal love such
Gorgeous buggery
Enduring litmus of beauty
Paragon of lost youth
Sliced clean through
Hacked quite away
Such a shame
You're so vain

New Oracles

Origins of
All cultures
Obscure beginning
Mist of myths
Fog of memory
Creation tales
Songs of heroes
Gilgamesh to Achilles
Burning bush of Moses
Sermon on the Mount
Ancient texts
Image, symbol to sign
Sinful semiotics
Convenience of
Alphabets
Sounds and syntax
Father to son
Oral traditions
Passed down
Then written
Power of scribes
Hundreds of Homers
Endless evangelists
Masters of text
High ranked officials
Chroniclers of kings
Suetonius on Caesars
Ancient Britain's Beowulf
India's Mahabharata
Carolingian Song of Roland
Einhard on illiterate Charlemagne

Abelard and Heloise
Tristan and Isolde
Love stories
Shang Dynasty's roasted turtles
Yarrow stalks of I Ching
Past looking to future
Searching for clues
Bible thumping preachers
Chapter and verse
As it written so shall it be
Battle cry of Allahu Akbar
Banzai shouts the Samurai
Edge of forest swamps ahead
The new unknown
Grateful dead
To be human in projective verse
Learning to breathe
Mother Earth
Speck of sand in the universe
Cosmology of galaxies beyond
Yet within us
Celestial navigations
Self rendered asunder
Fear and trembling
The horror of genocides
In each of us
Prattle of pundits
Talking heads decapitated
Headless horsemen
Sifting ashes covering asses
Future shock entrusted to poets

Sanskrit redux
Exquisite calligraphy
Spelling out chronicles of
Our ebb and flux

Sumerian Pop Quiz.

Vestal Virgins

Keepers of eternal flame
Honoring goddess Vesta
Guardian of hearth and home
Presiding over rituals
Pure and virtuous
Inspiration to all
Served from puberty
Some thirty years
Retired with pensions
Allowed to marry
Like Greek sibyls
Oracles and prophesies
Frenzied women
From whose mouths
The gods speak
Dire pronouncements
Too few listen
Matters and insights
Only women know
Prophets of doom
When men march to war
Bound for glory
Grim and gory
They sit and wait
Penelope at her loom
Through ebb and flow
The fairer sex
So soft and slow
Though father knows best
What comes next
Ignoring Virgin's hex

Paul Simon.

Little Richard

The '50s when
Rock was young
In the mirror
Primp and pomp
Before the prom
Squeezing zits
Squish splash
Stack of 45s
Life of the party
Buddy Holly
Fats Domino
Chuck Berry
Bo Diddley
The kicker
Little Richard's
Tutti Frutti
Shrill wail
Twist your frail
That crazy hair
Standing at piano
Not sitting down
Like Van Cliburn
Wild child
Sex machine
Got religion
Went straight
More or less
Maybe not
Caught him
Hanging with
Ron Wood

Still wicked cool
In shades
Dash of red
Sweating head
Feeling the heat
Flames of fame
Rock inferno
Incinerated
My generation

Little Richard in Shades.

Drummer Johny Barbata

Flight out of Frisco

Winging East

Home from the Coast

All that sunshine

Bit of chilly fog

Under Golden Gate Bridge

Vast Pacific facing Asia

Spotted him curbside

Dragging gear

Rod Stewart haircut

Too black to be honest

Still nicely thick

No need for a rug

Queued up behind us

Must be a rocker

Chirped with some aplomb

That's right mate

Drummer Johny Barbata

Whipping out his book

Sells stuff on the road

T-shirts, even signed sticks

Still Happy Together

Days with Turtles

Then Jefferson Airplane

After that Starship

Crosby, Stills, Nash & Young

Keeping the beat

Some hundred albums

Mostly studio sessions

Remembering Buddy Rich

Mentor and mutual friend

Headed for Oklahoma
Odd place between gigs
His wife's home
Remembering her fondly
Life on the road
Going it alone
Rock till you drop
Airport blues

On the road with rock drummer Johny Barbata.

Purple Rain

Odd juxtaposition
Rough and smooth
Royals in the news
Good and bad
Toast to the Queen at 90
Monarch since 1953
Before you were born
Photos of her brood
Shots of heirs
Would-be Kings
Toddler in short pants
Three steps down
Other headline
Not so great
Yet another exquisite corpse
The artist named Prince
Dead at 57
Such a short life
While seemingly indestructible
Keith rocks on borrowed time
Sunbathing in scorching heat of
Decadent celebrity while
That other Charles Prince of Wales
Patiently waits his coronation
Our royalty mostly spent
Sipping Earl Grey tea
Prince is dead
Hail to a purple reign

Pratfalls

Hey Pip it slipped
Off the cliff
Cousin Edward
An oddball misfit kid
Fingers stabbing our eyes
Maniacal laugh
Utterly deranged
Just kidding
Louise and I
Say it slipped to each other
Life off the rails
Free fall caterwauling through
Time and space
It slipped big time and how
Mistakes pile up
Near misses
Endless pratfalls
Chin music
Dodge ball
Things coming at us
Blistering speed
Daily challenges
Chaos theory
Getting back on the horse
Vocabulary of adversity
Threads of mishegoss
Woven into tapestries of
Quixotic reason
Drips and drabs off the chart
Fabricated as outsider art
Not making sense
Its own weird paradigm

Bonnie Prince Charlie

Limo sent round
Private jet to Heathrow
Then chopper to Scotland
Weekend at Balmoral Castle
In my usual room kilt laid out
Garish tartan of bold plaid
Colors of Sicilian clan
Bonnie Prince Charlie
To the mannerism born
His Highness in the library
Join him at three for tea
Rare Highland single malt
Exchanged greetings
Commonality of Charles
Recalling his birth
On the telly from Britain
Eight years after me
Took it quite personally
Younger brother and peer
Or so it has seemed
Meeting from time to time
Respecting strict protocols
Mutual interest in art
I reviewed his book
Watercolor landscapes
Gave it to Mom for Christmas
Not bad for an amateur
Talk about families
Children and heirs
Mum still on the throne
Brandy after dinner

Rising early for shooting
Me off my game
He bagged a few
Served that night
Roasted grouse and pheasant
Me as a peasant
Sharing the royal table
Woke up back home
Dreams of coronets
Swirling in my head
Memories of odd melancholy
The man who would be king

Royal Flush.

My Oldest Friend

Raeford Liles
Military family
Birmingham, Alabama
Fighter pilot South Pacific
Just a kid then
My oldest friend
This week 93
Wild and crazy guy
Brilliant collages
Godfather taught me
Survival skills
Laundry and cooking
Outrageous chef
Hotplate whipping
Up gourmet meals
In cold water flat
Seafood from markets
Near Port Authority
Hookers cruising
At night catching
Sailors and fish
Told bad jokes
Not always funny
He laughed anyway
Crazy as a coot
More lives than a cat
Having the last laugh

Coda

Paul Simon now 74
More or less my age
Has retired with no more ideas
Latest album his last
Stranger to Stranger
Bosh humbug
No end for artists
Not like my dad
A surgeon who withered away
Nothing left to say
Blade packed away
Late works so interesting
Deaf Beethoven and Goya
Haunting Ninth he couldn't hear
Prado's riveting Black Paintings
Heat-oppressed brain
Quite mad with pain
Monet at Giverny all but blind
As were Degas and Cassatt
What is that spirit
So charged to carry on
Into the beyond
So Paul you wimp
Shoot some hoops with
Julio in the schoolyard
Your despair a vast vacuum
Like Bowie's last Lazarus
Grim message that speaks to us
Show some respect for
That greatest rare gift
Art itself which has no meaning
Beyond being and nothingness

When I Grow Up

When you grow up
What do you want to be
They asked but that
Never happened
Grew up that is
Still Peter Pan or Charlie Brown
As Astrid calls me
Big Boy or The Big to friends
With a knowing laugh
Answer always changed
From cowboy to cop
Perhaps Superman
Wished I could fly
After first ballet Swan Lake
Ballet Russe de Monte Carlo
Briefly aspired to be a ballerina
It didn't last
Tutu to all that
Then Dad chimed in
He'll be a surgeon
Just like me
Chip off the old block
Bollocks it got ugly
Fist fight in the backyard
Ended up an artist
Whatever that means

Losing My Marbles

When I retired in 2005
Artist friend Thad Beal
Gave me a set of marbles
They came in a box
Nested in velvet
In case of mental emergency
Title on its cover
Amusing at the time
Significance didn't
Really sink in
Clever conceptual piece
Duchamp perhaps
Assisted Readymade
Like 50 cc's of Paris air
Lately however sure makes sense
Not just art object
Bit by bit losing it
More and more
Good to have backup
Them extra marbles
May come in handy
Someday all too soon

Matronly Mentor

Debbie was my friend
Rancid adolescence
My face exploding
Embarrassing volcanoes
Head awash in ideas
Randy loins
Liked her mother more
Regal Mrs. Gardner
British born Delphic Sybil
That lilting language
Redolent of class
Always reading
Home alone
When I went calling
Allegedly for her daughter
Neglectful husband
Rarely there
Stiff and proper
Venerable Yankee
Worked for IBM
Which seemed strange
Why would one
Spend their life
With business machines
More interesting things to do
Come in she would say
Offering her cold root beer
Home-made rarest treat
For a summer's day
Always a topic
Introduced she would say

Now Charles my dear
Curled up on the couch
Why are you studying Latin
Never thought of that
One just did
Labored through Caesar
Veni, vidi, vici
Then Cicero to Virgil
Catullus and the poets
Touch of Horace
You can't speak it
She argued
So what's the use
Stammered something
What I had been told
Ineptly rephrased
So in awe of her
Wit and wisdom
Hoping to please
Perhaps impress
So withered by our
Astute dialectics
Such delicious memory
Like that sweet beverage
Scion of Norwood Heights
Decades later I would tell her
Wish I paid more attention
To my Latin
Now desperately reading
Their fecund prose
Root of all syntax

Replete with wisdom
Insights of Empire
Rotting like a fish
From the head down
How like our own
Pining for Republic
Stoic noble Patricians
Or our founding fathers
Flawed indeed
Scamps and scoundrels
Seeking knowledge of
A decadent past
Now repeated
Through text
Retracing the steps
Such as it was
So shall it be

Rhinestone Cowboy

The day that country singer
Glen Campbell died
A picture by e-mail
Always amazing
Just incredible
Daily blasts
Links to obits
From Grand Old Opry
In that magic circle
Just like us
Relic of original theatre
Hallowed shrine
Fast Eddy posed
Alone in spotlight
Nashville nights
Backstage pass
Down home again
City of music
Whiskey and women
Where stars shine
Bright and true
Songs of America
Bringing him back
Time and again
Town that loves him
Like a native son
Which he is in
More ways than one
Through and through
Red white and blue
To all us kids
Loyal and true

Young Sturgeon

Like himself Dad
Wanted me to be a surgeon
Downright insisted on it
Him and me in the OR
Side by side
Gowned and gloved
Blood and guts
Masterful incisions
As he demonstrated
From time-to-time
More often than not
Passing out or throwing up
Beat some sense in me
When I refused
No Dad says I
Full of defiance
When I grow up
Want to be a sturgeon
Master of sturgery
Following in your finsteps
Wet and wild
Flipping all about
Frolicking night and day
Sleek as all getout
Slicing through water
Cool as a flipper
Making mighty waves
Hey Dad look at me
Free as can be
Much more fun
Than slicing up stuff

Where's the laughs in that
Bloody hell mate
Much better to
Be a blimey fish
Friggin' Beluga caviar
Slipping down real nice
Flutes of champagne
Playing a merry tune
Laughing at the moon
With just sixpence to
Call me own

A young sturgeon.

Met at the Met

Cantankerous guy
Troublemaker
Famously cussed out
Carl Andre an ersatz liberal
Gallery talk over the top
Passionate idealist
Boston artist Michael Russo (1908–1990)
One of my guys
Loved a fellow paisan
Wrote his essay
Mass Art retrospective which
Jeff Keough curated
Years ago March 1981
He studied at Yale
Returned to art
Middle-aged in 1960
Years on the lam
Union organizer
Card-carrying member
Communist Party
Freedom fighter
Era of McCarthyism
Lives lost and ruined
Then as now
When black lives matter
As Assad slaughters
His own people
Nothing changes
Undaunted
Mike recalled
Best and worst people

In the party
All over America
Small towns
Cheap hotels
Mills and factories
In NY sought refuge
Sanctuary in the Met
Quiet afternoons
Safe from FBI
Not art lovers
Roaming around
Ran into a dame
Didn't catch her name
Never asked
They would meet
Look at pictures
Go for coffee
Chat and hang out
Stunning blonde
They talked about art
Married to a playwright
She said discreetly
Ever so sweetly
Remained anonymous
Yes of course
It was Marilyn
He said with a glow
Speaking of long ago
To and fro with Michelangelo
Through rooms with a view

Mississippi Blues Man Mose Allison

Out of Ole Miss
Grew up on country blues
Sardonic sophistication
Crooning slur
Seductive drawl
Twisted sound
Bitch-slamming lyrics
Glommed onto
Prestige albums
Back Country Suite
Creek Bank
Autumn Song
Back in the `50s
My main man
Mose Allison
Piano sounded
Both modern
Post bop
But down home
Cornpone soul
That week at Sandy's
Sparse house
More love than money
Me as MC
During breaks
Fell by the bar
Glass of milk
So odd for a blues man
Clean and sober
Slick as a snake
Fangs in your heart

Seventh son in
Whole wide world
There was only one

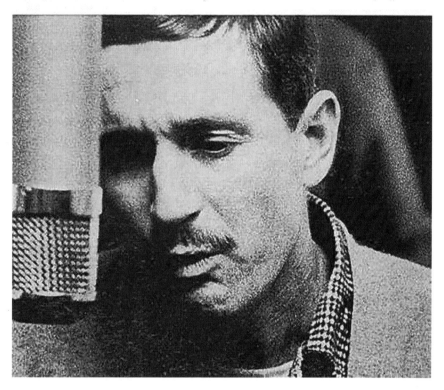

CREEK BANK / MOSE ALLISON

Two Lennys: Bruce and Bernstein

Double exposure
Teenage years
Two Lennys
Not joined at the hip
One was Lenny Bruce
The other wasn't
Lenny Bernstein
Connected to both
Bruce the ultimate hipster
Outrageous humor
The other guy
Odd connection
Like me Bernstein
Grew up in Brookline
But attended
Boston Latin School
Where masters
Years later recalled
Practicing piano
His score for
West Side Story
Brought class
To Broadway
Then Hollywood
Bruce hounded
To junkie death
Killed by censors
Acid insights
Scorching America's dreams
Talking dirty
Bernstein's demise

Gracing the podium
Fame and fortune
Less poetic elide
Smokes, booze and boys
Both off the rails
Odd influences
Yin and Yang
Forks in the road
Don't fake it
Not fade away

A profile of Leonard Bernstein.

Autodidact

Madison Square Garden
Horse show
Just a teenager Jim Jacobs
Rider of the Purple Sage
Young scholars
Museum of Fine Arts
Adjoining offices
He Greek me Gyppo
So many phases
Plots and subplots
Alice's Breast Flaunt
Tales of Mt. Shango
Ski to surf
Flute to cello
Gamesmanship
He can do anything
Laughed about it
Yesterday at lunch
Annual meeting
Flew in to
North Adams Airport
On the run as usual
Talked about minimalism
Made his fortune curating shows
Mnuchin Gallery
Ryman, LeWitt, Andre
Started with Judd's
Stacked boxes
Aesthetic precision
Clean and pure
Lean and mean

Visual information
Apollonian
Like classical Greeks
Remembering
Four hundred dinners
Judd and Chamberlain
Best friends
Heavy drinkers
Not Jim though
Lightweight he
Called himself
Asked how to do
All those things
Like sound guy
On the road with Lou
First gig from Bernie who
Managed Baez
Concert at Sing Sing
Manning the board
Scared stiff
Faking it
Huge laugh
Can you imagine
Con among cons
King Con
Ultimate apeshit
If you are reasonably
Smart and hip
You can master any job
In about two years
He explained

Except Pope or President
What about Trump I asked
Ultimate twofer
Great ape for sure
Jim barfed his lunch
What a hoot
Flew home
Same time next year
Like when on the road
We passed in the west
Talked by cell phone
He headed to
Colorado and we
Home to the Berkshires
From Four Corners
Somewhere in Kansas
No time to stop
Zooming by
Life in the fast lane
Me a bit slower
La vida loca

Grateful Dead

Packed away
Box opened
Light of day
Two heads
Real ones
Dad's now ancient
Med school
Surgeon studying anatomy
Fascinated me growing up
Taking lid off looking inside
Moving jaw up and down
When young intern at MFA
Egyptian Department
Basement with mummies
Bought a Tibetan skull bowl
Used for drinking blood
Reminders of mortality
Odd artifacts
Memento mori
Grim reapers

What Of It

What's to be done
Well you might ask
But why indeed
Edward Albee has died
Not afraid of him anymore
Fear eats itself
Isn't that true Martha
Let's all get the guests
Intruders on our privacy
Such as it is
Ever muddled by outsiders
Tramping on petunias of
Inner lives
Vast emptiness pretty vacant
Filling up with
Sand and mud
Mundane everyday
Measured in teaspoons
To and fro yo Michelangelo
Casual conversations
Meaningless encounters
Lives half lived
Ambitions plunged to earth
Icarus fallen into the sea
Washed ashore corpse on beach
Winged defeat of Samothrace
Tropical island
Some odd place
Frenetic pace
Dim memory in your face
Up yours muthah Fuggah

What we thought
It might be
Sea to shining sea
When the sun never set
On you or me

Private art dealer, Jim Jacobs, also answers to Shango.

Astrid in London.

Making Book

Gray light through tall windows
Early winter in the loft
Heavy snow today
Off to Stowe this weekend
Holiday celebration
Gift to share then
Settled in yet again
Starting another book
Recalling efforts of
First four now one more
Where to begin
All those poems last two years
Random and chaotic
Trying to make sense
Finding threads
Connecting themes
Trashing stuff
Not everything wonderful
Brutal triage of once timely
Yesterday's newspapers
Wrapping stinking fish
Like fucking Trump
Bonfire of the vanities
Honing in on universals
What lasts forever
When we are long gone
Eye of newt tongue of bat
A witch's brew of soup and stew
Long dark months rich with dreams
When Persephone sleeps with Hades
Until hell freezes over

Topsy Turvy

Steady drip of fine sand
Measuring our lives
Sanguine youth now
More bottom than top
Once shit for brains
Raging hormones
Outrageous daredevils
Death defying stunts
Hope and dreams
Then even-steven
Measured midpoint
Family and career
Hunkered down
Flummoxed flip-flop
Reflective reversal
Topsy turvy running amuck
Cooking a perfect egg
Neither hard nor soft
That's no yoke
Tricks of memory
Not making sense
Too much history
Friggin' millennials
So self absorbed
Just as we were
Buried under shifting dunes
Beneath a canopy of stars
So distant and confounding
Spaced out oddity
Vox clamantis in deserto
Nobody hears and now

Here and Now

What are you doing here
Got the same call
Doing what I was told
Please don't scold
That's getting old
Just obey orders of the day
So they say but hey
Why the heck not
Nothing else to do
Wasn't always that way
Fighting with all my might
Too old for that now
Know what I mean
Making the scene
That's for kids
Hey just go with the flow
Makes more sense
The marvelous vista
Or should I say overview
Where I can see for
Miles and miles and miles
Who knew

Time After Time

What time is it you asked
In the waiting room
Said a perfect stranger
Actually nobody is perfect
Or truly strange
How very timely
My watch just stopped
Self-winding Omega
With mind of its own
Jolted awake from sleep
Perchance to dream
Why are you here
I asked the stranger
Becoming more familiar
Hardly a friend
Keeping a distance
Here for tests she said
Oh, I see same with me
Drawing buckets of blood
Then I have to go
Where and when she asked
Over there then someplace else
That makes sense
Perhaps or maybe not
Pitter patter small talk
But hey none of my business
You know how it is
Here today gone tomorrow
Say have a nice day
Don't be a stranger
I hear you but do I really
Does anyone actually
Give a damn

High Noon

Open Carry
Paranoia prevails
Armed to the teeth
Packing heat
Everyday downtown
Business as usual
Right to bear arms
Backed by Congress
Anytime anywhere
Grocery shopping
Housewives with pistols
Or pepper spray
Plus mace in your face
Just in case
Trigger happy mishaps
Tempers flare
Scores settled
On the spot
Cops and robbers
Corpses piled high
Daily body count
Like on TV
Vietnam in the '60s
The killing
Here and now

Wright or Wrong

Vintage Brahmin Boston
City of cod and snobs
Beantown where Irish
Need not apply
Blue bloods
Thin-lipped
Narrow-minded
Sons of a bitch
Of Liberty
Who can say
Back in the day
Distinguished visitor
Outspoken architect
Frank Lloyd Wright
Addressing venerable
Copley Society
Caused shock waves
When he said
What Boston needs
Is one hundred
First-class funerals
That was then
But what about now
Difference between
Wright and wrong

Solid Gold Commode

Having to go
At the Guggenheim
Winding down the ramp
Gliding past art
Always unwinding
Bladder bursting
Feeling the urge
Miniscule toilets
At intervals
The Wright stuff
During the ascent
From top down
Unisex affairs
Tiny water closets to
Do your thing
If one is busy
Move to the next
Wait a minute
Why the long line
Roped off
Guard up front
Can this be
A work of art
Have to see
Curiosity got best of me
Wait not worth it
Time and tide
Moved on a bit
Glanced back
Only four in queue
Gave it a shot

Two women
Quit and left
Moved up
Heard a flush
Then my turn
Burst in
There it was
Solid gold commode
Cattelan calls it America
Tried to lift the seat
No luck
My aim was true
Lingered a bit
What a relief
Absorbed the experience
Rudely absurd
Recalled Duchamp
R. Mutt's urinal
Dubbed Fountain
Pissed people off
Truly treasured
Dada prank
Same idea now
More extravagant
Picking up my coat
Exclaimed to guards
Black and Hispanic
I just took a piss
In a pot of gold
They laughed
Leaning in one said

That's America
Sure is I replied
Going to hell
In a solid gold
Crapper
Old Glory as
Wasteland

There were long lines at the Guggenheim Museum.

Up in Smoke

Rooster crowed
First light
Crept over horizon
Gray morning
Overcast in
Every sense
Dragged from cells
Lined up in front of
Chipped wall
Revolution crushed
Mass executions
Presiding major
With compassion
Offered last cigarettes
Prisoner lit up
Inhaled with gulps
That soothing
Narcotic nicotine
The second refused
I'm trying to quit
The third asked
With intensity
Do you have any
Medical marijuana
Nice to get a buzz
Go out on a high
Rifles cracked
That was that

After the Rain

Sticking my head up
From the crater
We leaped into
Yesterday during
The thick of it
Scorched earth
Barren landscape
Forest reduced to splinters
Stark and beautiful
Against moody sky
Acrid air burning our lungs
Looking about for
Signs of life
From under you said
I'm hungry
Perhaps a carrot
Foraging in the muck
Now what you asked
What's to be done
Are we alone
Will it happen again
Crawling out crouched in pain
No broken bones
Pulling you along
Where are we going
You asked plaintively
Not really sure
Wish I could say more
No point staying here
Perhaps we'll find food
Get in out of rain

Abandoned homes
In village ahead
From there to where
Tomorrow is another day
Let the children play

Morphed Growth Rings. Astrid Hiemer photo.

Checkout Counter

Fill out forms
List of meds
Take a number
Sit on bench
How many ahead
Old magazines
Christmas issues
In summer
Droning TV
Stupid talk show
Background noise
Trying to read
Book of plays
O'Neill project
One after another
Theatrical blur
Measuring time
Teaspoons in a cup
Watch it buster
Finger pricked
Twice a day
Distracted reverie
Who went next
Into the office
Hey friggin lady
Came after me
Crank up cell phone
Check e-mail
Stock market
Red Sox lost again
Lousy pitching

Trivial distractions
Until big time
Our card gets
Punched

Ben and Jerry. Astrid Hiemer photo.

Surfing Tsunami

Bing bang boom
Clusters of bad luck
Assaults on the senses
Seemingly casual conversations
Artist enduring setbacks
Health, creative, financial
Now divorcing
Where to go from here
Possibly Canada
If Trump wins
Couple of days later
Interaction with lawn guy
Salt of the earth
Great dad works six jobs
Supports as many kids
Three from her prior
Tearing up the sheets
Devastated he mows grass
By dawn's early light learn
She again cheated death
Emergency room
terrible accident not long ago
Banged up old friend
Punk rocker now has
Breast cancer
Then call from Robert
Mentioned my poem
Shooting in the Ranks
They're at it again
Rasta philosopher
Massive heart attack

Gone no visitors
Tsunami of mayhem
Crashing over us
No Beach Boys tune
For this Surfin Safari
Riding the waves
Wipeout

Spirit Boat.

First Light

Bolt upright
Deep in night
End of sleep
Stumble in the dark
Kitchen and coffee
Far too early
Cell phone
Not charging
Last e-mail
Poet friend Stephen
Medical emergency
Now OK
Wilma wrote
Again our mortality
Catching us by surprise
So many close calls
Too much on our plate
Dawn brought
The Eagle on our lawn
Shuffled out to get it
Stiff leaning down
Distraction of news
Lasting a few minutes
Sports and politics
Fleeting interests
Compared to big picture
Not very pretty
Once an illusion
Brightening day
Melts the shadows
Making midnight thoughts

Seem moot compared to
Gentle unfolding
Another summer day
Painted with colored light
Things that crawl at night
Gone by dawn

Twin Lights, Gloucester, Massachusetts.

Encyclopedia vs. Wikipedia

Age of the Enlightenment
Gathering all knowledge
Volumes of Encyclopedia
Read aloud in salons
Doomed Ancien Regime
Eager to know what
Denis Diderot and
Jean le Rond d'Alembert
Wrote about those
Whose heads would roll
Exciting Sans-culottes
Vengeful vulgarians
Pen mightier than the sword
Voltaire said for the few
Knowledge as power
Freedom of speech
Yet easily squandered
Reduced to blather
Gossip as journalism
Libel and lies
Ersatz fake news
In the '50s Dad bought
Encyclopedia Britannica
Once so valued now
Moldering in our basement
Callously trashed
Tossed in the dumpster
Triage of downsizing
Now all online
Just Google it
All hail Wikipedia

So much speedier
The Age of Reason as
Collateral damage
Bombarded by CNN
Where now are the Philosophes
Their modest proposals
Words of wit and wisdom
Instead a strident screed
Pretending to be news
Trash-talking revolution
So called social mediocrity
Off with our heads

False Door.

Gloom and Doom

Dark clouds
Rolling thunder
Long shadows
Hard times
Gloom and doom
No he said sharply
It's gloom or doom
One or the other
Oh really
Thought it was ok
Who's to say
Matter of how
You see things
Like Sarah Palin
Looking at Russia
From her porch
Sky is falling
Bad stuff
Creeping over us
Poison ivy
In the berry patch
Mayhem at the mall
What happened to
Have a nice day
Let the children play
Armageddon then Heaven
Hell is other people

Future Shock

Uncanny how past often
More vivid than present
Decades old trivia
Incidents in vivid detail
The look of a room
What people said
Mood of the moment
Etched in memory
Evidence of life
Sifted through
Ordering legacy
While yesterday
Or even an hour ago
But a blur
Books fresh read
Too soon forgotten
Titles and authors
Washing over our
Waves of insights
Crashing on rocks
Jumble of vignettes
Tossed and tumbled
Put through ringer
Bleached by scorching
Glare of Catholic Guilt
Confessed back then
Forgotten only to sin again
Mobius stripped a
Space shuttle at warp speed
Ultimate voyage
Beyond our horizon

Dissent

Rules meant to be broken
Rude and outrageous
Clever assassin
Artists as Oedipus
Killing all ancestors
Lost civilizations
Wife/mother as muse
What's your excuse
Sister/daughter
Blinded exiles
Cost of creation
Phoenix from ashes
Not making sense
Just do the work
Three-chord punks
Making rough music
Trashed and scorned
Flame-out failures
Facing enemy as self
Bloodied by art wars
Stench of dead art
Some live to tell the tale
Retire with medals
Nurse their wounds
Unearthed eons later
Lust morphed to dust
Destroying temples and museums
Mausoleums of memory
Zero tolerance for
Easy bourgeois art

Before and After

Dramatic change
Day and night
The ugly before
Nip and tuck
Beautiful after
Ponce de Leon
Fountain of Youth
Perhaps Florida
Special diet
Kelp and kale
Yukky stuff
No burgers and fries
Frenetic exercise
Sweat equity
You look maaarvelous
With faint praise
Meaning that
You didn't previously
Old fat and ugly
Obscene obesity
Lose twenty pounds
Folks will say
You're just fabulous
So what about before
Back when you pretended
To like your fat friend
So long ago when
I was young and svelte
But pretty stupid

Basta

Lawn party yesterday
Gorgeous under the tent
Italian lady loved theatre
We discussed a production
Cat on a Hot Tin Roof
Agreed it was terrible
More travesty than tragedy
Probing deeper
She admires Miller
More enduring universal themes
Did you see
View from the Bridge
On Broadway
A brilliant deconstruction
To Williams I added
Eugene O'Neill
So repetitious she observed
Dated content
No controversy today
Same story over and over
Consumed by self
How many lives
Do we have I asked
Sensing a trap
Cautiously answered
One of course
Exactly
The great artists
Eat themselves
Cannibals their
Guts stuffed into

Sausage consumed
By audiences
Same old stories
No more flesh on bones
Their last works
Gasps of dust
Ashes-to-ashes
The greatest ones
As exquisite corpses
Discussed during lunch
With she who could
Care less for artists

Garden Sculpture.

Modern Lovers

They met online
Exchanged images
Texted intense messages
Mutual attraction
Explored interests
Thumbs blazing words
Staccato semiotics
Finally met at Starbucks
Dutch treat of course
Hooking up for sex
Over lattes never spoke
Just kept texting
No awkward conversation
Easier that way
Clean and concise
Wordplay far too messy
Exchanged glances
Tapping out romance
Ended with C u ltr
I luv u 2
They married
Had three kids
Never uttering a word
A perfect mom
Eventual empty nesters
Just like u

Montezuma's Revenge

When in Mexico
Don't drink the water
No fresh salads
First time in Europe
Surprised by
Pellegrino at restaurants
Why pay for what's free
All that plastic
Now clogging landfills
Floating in oceans
Cheap gallon jugs
For residents of
Flint drinking lead
From old pipes
Even nearby
Hoosick Falls
Where upstate
The air is clean
But the water ain't
Coming soon
To a community
Near you
Not safe to
Turn on the tap
Montezuma
Coming soon
To our town

Perhaps

You might think that
Who's to say
Right or wrong
Matter of opinion
Too many easy answers
Most prefer simplicity
Nothing complicated
Cut to the chase
Get to the point
What do you mean
Where do I sign
Will it hurt
How long will it last
When will I be
Well again
Perhaps never
Get used to it
Just the way it is
No use complaining
Suck it up
Get with the program
Come back in three weeks
Stay on the meds
Call if you have problems
We're there for you
Rest assured
Or maybe not
How may we
Direct your agita

Mangia Bene

I would eat anything
That didn't eat me first
Boston's North End
Sicilian neighbors
Local eatery for lunch
Phil Bleeth visiting
With a twinkle I ordered
Pigskins over pasta
Like rolled footballs
Made a great show
Mmm alla casalinga
With a laugh then said
Can't eat this crap
He howled at my prank
When dining Chinese
Order extra MSG
Heavy on gluten please
Lay on soy and carbs
Four ears of corn
Slathered with butter
In the summer
The good old days
Now pills for breakfast
No more fun
Not getting high
Just staying alive
Fear eats soul food
Fools die young
With shit eating grins

As Time Goes By

Greatest Generation
World at war
Fear of the Bomb
By the 1950s
Dreams of the Future
Disney's Tomorrowland
Selling us fantasy of
Man on the Moon
Autorama pitching
Cars with fins
Dad's gaudy Cadillac
Baby blue convertible
Mom's a three-toned Dodge
Venus wore fur
First frozen food
Peas in winter not canned
Status symbols
Better times on horizon
Science and technology
Promise of a better day
Now not all that great
It was so simple then
Time for family gatherings
Saying Grace before
Home-cooked meals
Dad making sauce
No fast food
Radio before television
Primitive yet galvanic
Them was the days before
Glut of media

Obscene politics
World again teetering on
Xenophobic global migrations
Returned full circle
What our patriotic parents
Fought and died for
A now that seems
Not as great as before

Clover. Astrid Hiemer photo.

Zig and Zag

Quandry of whether
To zig or zag
Hang with the gang
Me and me mates
Bunch of reprobates
To cut loose or
Go with the flow
Perhaps to be but
Not for me
Unquestionably
Without a doubt
Neither here nor there
Hair today gone tomorrow
Guys bald as eggshells
Smooth as silk
Shiny pates no hairy apes
So it seems more or less
Then a fork in the road
Taking it
Path less followed
Way out West
Gold in them thar hills
Or right back here
My own backyard
Drawing a line in sand
Taking a stand
For something or other
Do the right thing
God on my side
Truth Justice and
The American Way

Leaping tall buildings
In a single bound
World hovering on edge
What's to be done
Heads or tails
Stop making sense
So what the heck
All loosey goosey
Grim Reaper what you sow
Later man gottah go

Ski Tracks. Astrid Hiemer photo.

Riff and That

Rumble in the jungle
Screeching birds
Great ape lumbering about
Brush shattered
Crashing sounds
Swooping arms
Whooshing by
Close call
Duck for cover
Break for clearing
Circle wagons
Hunker down
Defensive posture
Zooooom
There it is again
Piercing the air
Tropical torment
Lush and rank
Blistering heat
Blaze of glory
Good grief
On the run
Race for the river
Dive under
Swim for life
Maybe make it
Washed up
Panting on shore
Deep breaths
Heart racing
Tapping a beat

On brittle ribs
Skeletal vibraphone
Anxious mallets
Crazy rhythm
Mayhem swing
Bop cacophony
Utter panic
Looking up
Long and deep
Canopy of sky
Through and blue
Wondering why

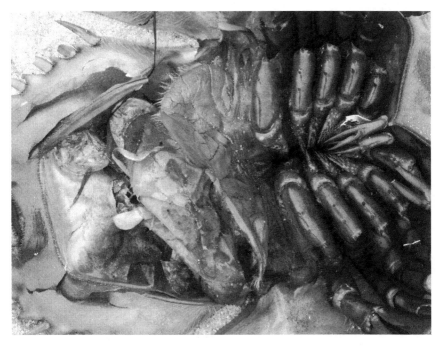

Horseshoe Crab. Astrid Hiemer photo.

High Heat

Gonzo poets
Like boys of summer
On the mound throwing high heat
Brush back pitches
A little chin music
Reader kissing dirt
Painting the corners
A Rembrandt with
Nobody on full count
Catcher flipping signs
Framing the plate
Right down the pike
Whiffing them
Flailing for meaning
Sardonic confidence
Total control of my game
Pennant fever baby
Cranking out books
Grand slam over Green Monster
Fourth season as starter
As many books
Nearing All Star break
Stats off though
Hitters waiting on fastball
Not zipping past
More reliant on changeup
Bounced out of rotation
Ten years in the pen
Not for me late innings
Covering weddings and funerals
Smiles of a summer day

Apocalypse stuff wears thin
Nobody gives a fig
About infinity
Never did though
Losing the edge
No pigeons in the park
New Yorker's poets
For the smarty set
Go down swinging
Still wild and crazy
Or some shit like that
Yeah I mean you buster
Heart of darkness
In the cave with Kurtz

Cactus. Astrid Hiemer photo.

On the Move

Middle of semester
Bought first home
East Boston triple-decker
Huge backyard
Cheap but funky move from
People's Republic of Cambridge
To Maverick Square
Raw and ethnic
Great taco stands
But no bookstores
Weekends loading the car
Sunday nights totally pooped
Final push friends helped
Boxes everywhere
Welter of confusion
Everything packed
Lost the final exams
Told my boss
You did what Bill asked
Sorry I lost them
As well as my mind
Finally there with
Towels for curtains
No light in the halls
Flashlights groping about
Car outside packed with stuff
Went missing
Likely culprit a friend
Of badass neighbors
Needed ride home
Welcome to the neighborhood
They laughed back before
Webster Street was gentrified

Swamp Talk

Slithering about
Through muck
Reeking swamp
Eyes above surface
Perusing for prey
Mean and hungry
Slim pickings
Next to golf course
Occasional lost soul
Puppy perhaps
Gone astray
Snapped up
Quick as a flash
Relentless tormentor
No friend of mine
Swamp lizard
Laying in wait
Ready to pounce
Jaws clenched
Death roll
Dragging us under
Lunchmeat
Guised as debate
Screed of insults
While a bird
Screeched warnings
Tread lightly
Near this creature
Intent on mayhem
Killing machine
Alligator hide
Deflecting all
Reason

Floral Oracle

Giant daisy
Fresh and white
Pride of summer
Petals plucked
Odd and even
Familiar mantra
She loves me
She loves me not
Either or
Youthful romance
So different now
When we know
Answers
No need to
Damage flowers
Consult oracles
Eternal love
Tested by time
Blooms in us

Bald Eagle

Dawn broke
Over the forest
From bed of pine needles
Looking up through branches
Mosaic of sky
Bald eagle landed on my chest
Menacing gaze
Chiseled beak but
Not like Prometheus
My liver spared
Winged predator
Tore at flesh
Ripped out heart
Devoured soul
Consumed by flame
Feathers blazing
Flash of heat
Turned to dust
Transformed
Now Icarus
Soared toward sun
Swooped over earth
Filled with
Great spirit

Depression Glass

What to keep or sell
Garage sale
Getting rid of stuff
Treasures and trash
Decades ago
Revere Flea Market
Started collecting
Depression glass
Real cheap
Parent's generation
Newlyweds
Dish night
At the movies
Hard times
Quite beautiful
We used it
Everyday ware
Fancy plates
For dinner parties
Investment back then
For rainy day
Worth a fortune
Well not really
Didn't sell
Even for a buck
No luck

Redux

How come
What do you mean
The thing
What thing
You know
The thing
Oh really
Not that again
No really
No way
Oh come on
Why bother
Because
You know
It's the thing
Over and over
Again and again
How absurd
Same old same old
That's the thing
Of it

Pendulum

Glorious fall
More like summer
Brilliant foliage
Toasty days
Then kebam
Mood swing
Snow and slush
Mucking about
Before Halloween
Cripes criminy
Not ready for this
Sloshing to Joy's Sushi House
Weekly gathering
First a few of us then
More stomped in
Festive gathering
Getting our fix
Wonton and gossip
Merry banter
Margaritas all around
Just five bucks
Best in the Berkshires
Snowbirds departing
Some long gone
Ranks getting thin
Ever more intimate
Dark side of moon
Into the night
Sloppy streets
Puddle hopping
Shoes soaked then

Sound sleep
Snug as a bug in a rug
With dreams of spring

Snowbirds Departing. Astrid Hiemer photo.

Raven

Things we say
But do not mean
Truth or dare
Game of life
Tossing dice
Coming up
Snake-eyes
Crapping out
Rolling thunder
From down under
Shiver and shake
Brutal earthquake
Groping for chakra
Spinal tap
Inner oasis
Crossing deserts
Dates and tea
Beneath
Shading trees
Burning sands
Blistered feet
Dude ranch
Tenderfoot
Kemosabe
Not so savvy
Queen for a day
Tears of joy
Bathed in bathos
Crocodile weeps
For Byzantium
Shimmering gold

Breaching leviathan
Swarthy Levantine
Ripping magic carpet
Out from under
Legerdemain
Rending asunder
Shredded sails
Catch no breeze
Cast adrift
Painted oceans
Marooned
Lost souls
Down under
Evermore

Flatboatmen and the Shark.

Ameliorate

Troubled waters
Recent turmoil
Sleepless nights
So much agita
Roar of bad news
Reduced to a ripple
No tsunami
Crashing on our
Holiday beach
Just the two of us
Home alone
Loving it
Special celebration
Sharing turkey breast
With fixins
Squash and sweet potatoes
Gatherings across America
Hopefully serene
Truce for the day
On this occasion
Having less to say
Lots of small talk
Games played
Scores discussed
Superbowl odds
Winter trades
Stuffing the gut
Full to bursting
Then a snooze
Sanctuary
From storm outside

Wild winds
Reduced to whispers
Apple pie and mother
A time when lions
Lay down with lambs
Pause for
Peace in our Kingdom
Rare day when
Nothing happens
But football

Astrid on the beach at Markland, Nova Scotia.

Trash Talk

"No one but a blockhead ever wrote except for money."
Dr. Samuel Johnson

These words
Sorry Dr. Johnson
A work of art
Gift from me to you
My life actually
Spelled out line for line
Not for sale
No tangible value
Just thoughts
Mad rantings
Over morning coffee
In the Berkshires gray day
First of many winter setting in
Thinking of all of you
Shadows cast over me
From then to now
School chums
Old girlfriends
All kinds of pals
Tons of artists
Jazz musicians
Sweet nights in sad cafes
Pugs and thugs
Dead hipsters
Gonzo poets
Piled high
Heaps of memories
Of no value

No secondary market
Even Jim Jacobs
Can't sell this
Like Dylan
Plan to ignore Nobel Prize
No trip to Sweden
White tie and tails
These tales are free
Just scribbles
Comments on Decline of Empire
Raped earth gasping for air
No purchase price
Worth less than two cents
Kiss someone you love
Do it for me
All one can hope for
Thundering accolades
Enigmatic fame game
Consumes our soul
Inferno of striving
Me, me, look at me
Better to give it away
Box of memories
Dumped at Goodwill
Schmattas that matter
For time evermore

Building Walls

Poe's Masque of the Red Death
Pasolini's film Salò
120 Days of Sodom
Boccaccio's Decameron
Fortified against
Camus' The Plague
Within the walls
Danse Macabre
Safe and contained
So it seemed
Ultimate insiders
Outside now
Mexicans/Aliens
All those not
Straight, white
God-fearing Christians
Everyone else as others
Open season
Bagged and tagged
Deported in millions
Families divided
Young black men
Slaughtered by cops
Muslims vilified
Klan burning crosses
Protests turned ugly
Hauling down Confederacy
In Charlottesville
Days of rage
Nothing new
China's Great Wall

Hadrian's in Britain
Keeping out Scots
Uncouth highlanders
Pax Romana
Never works
Our turn now
Burning bridges
Neo isolationism
Shadow boxing
Plato's The Cave
The rot within
Souls consumed
Drowning in venom
Toxic paranoia
Xenophobia
Old as time
Hic transit dracones
Fear eats itself
All is vanity

Static

Endless chatter
Assault on America
Idiotic Tweets
Attacks on all things
Human and decent
National pride
Race, religion, gender
Sense of fair play
Pigs at the trough
Elephants actually
Ravenous appetites
Gorging themselves oink oink
Bloated gout of privilege
Blinded by greed
Blithering screed of hate
Death dance of oligarchs
Bait and switch opportunism
Taking food off the table
Of decent God-fearing folks
Not all zealots or Xenophobes
Trivial compared to
Space-time continuum
Blip on the radar screen
Obliterating real issues
Survival of the species
Air we breathe water to drink
Legacy of future generations
Trashed with swipes of the pen
Held up for all to see
Hey world look at me
Mad and vile

Not worth shit
Last days of the Republic
We too will fall
No Chicken Little
Oblivion of all that
Once was great
E pluribus no longer unum

Beach Detritus. Astrid Hiemer photo.

Fission

Family and friends
Our loved ones
Ties that bind
Cradle to grave
Tried and true
Tested by time
Links of commonality
Life experiences
Disruptive words or deeds
Taking sides on
Political divide
World gone mad
Drifting apart
Calls not made
Natural erosion
Slip sliding away
Or emotional explosion
Smashed and bashed
Violent disruption
Split to smithereens
Gaping wounds
Critical distances
Cracked at the seams
What does it mean
Milk of human kindness
Gorilla glue plugging holes
Binding up splinters
Oozing into cracks
Sticky stuff
Knitting us together
Lessons learned

Making new history
No more samosamo
Hardly pristine
All patched up
Rough and ugly not
Pretty as a picture
Perhaps better stronger
From here to eternity
Moving on or letting go

Mirage.

Humbled by Hubble

Uncertainty principle
Utterly flattening Newton
Medieval notions of God
Jerusalem as center of Universe
When maps were flat
For most folks still are
Even Lutherans
One nation under
God of carnage
Comical chaos not so
Funny as endless space
Hubble nearing its end
Gazing ever deeper
Making us seem smaller
Puny dunes of sand
Stars and galaxies
Twinkle twinkle
Numerous as grains on
All the world's beaches
Sons of beaches on beaches
Oceans of notions
Queer as folk
Peaches for preachers
Bullies in pulpits
Me as picador
Banderillero's barbs
Enraging bourgeois beast
Swipes of the cape
Blood on the sand of time
Hell as other people
Pusillanimous pugilists

Ropeadopers
Ali set me free
Arms too short to box with God
Mud wrestle with infinity
Again you scoffed
As is your want or shuck
Jive and jitter
Gary Glitter in Quadrophenia
Roman candle whoosh
Shot in the dark
Lighting night sky
What best to say
Depends on the day
Quoting all those sources
Better and wiser ones
Artists must ignore
Stay true to their work
Robbed from the masters
So says the savant
Pleading sly ignorance
Godhead or is it
Brideshead revisted
All them slimy limeys
Guardians of the canon
Fodder for gonzo
Sound and fury
Signifying here and now
Slip sliding away
As Tonto would say
Eh Kemosabe

Movie Night on Bald Mountain

Sensual summer evening
Sultry under stars
Tanglewood lawn packed
Blankets spread
Yet again John Williams
Conducting iconic scores
With Andris Nelsons
Clips of swashbucklers
Slashing swords
Flashes of bygone times
Movie Night
Later roiled in sleep
Tossing turmoil
Making art
A frequent theme
Struggles so acute
With my father
Ever menacing
Chiding me fiercely
Intimate encounters
Friends and enemies
Itchy slights to
Scratch and sniff
Glimmering glances
Magnified in restless sleep
Looming ever larger
Epic works mocked
My best efforts
Wrecked by morning's light
What might have been
Poof by dawn

Torn up hopes
Tussled sheets
Tsunami dreams
Morning coffee
Catching up on news
Online the latest threats
Unfolding disasters
The human comedy
Not terribly funny
Dick Gregory died
Remembering him
Backstage chat
Before his fade to black
Escape hatch of
Bursting fantasies
Flares in the air
Curious memories
Thinking back to
Early days of TV
Walking to movies on
Saturday afternoons
Along Beacon Street
To Cleveland Circle
Closer to home or
Coolidge Corner further away
A long trek to Brighton
Now and then for matinees
Near St. Elizabeth's Hospital
Tomb like Egyptian
Decades before basement
Dark and dusty MFA

Surrounded by mummies
Venerable colleagues
Silent friends
Grateful Dead
There I saw exotic
King Solomon's Mines
Most exciting movie ever
Such a thrill to see
Debonair Stewart Granger
Most handsome man alive
How I loved movie stars
Most of the pretty boys
Not very good actors
That hardly mattered
No such thing as bad
More sponge than critic
Soaking up adventures
Thrill of being there
Alone in the dark
Escapes from dad
With better things
For me to do
My very own world
Not about cinema
That pretentious word
Or Parisian Film Noir
Cahiers du Cinéma term
For black and white
So friggin' pretentious
Cagney and Bogart
Edgar G. Robinson as Little Caesar

Thugs and gangsters
Dillinger, Machine Gun Kelly
Before Bonnie and Clyde
Say hello to my little friend
When color was rare era of grisaille
Then Cinerama with curtains parting
Widening the screen
Making movies bigger and better
Caught up by epics
Occasional trip downtown
By rattler across the tracks
To Washington Street
Its glare of marquees
Crying out to me
Vortex of films swirling within
Home for dinner
Never revealing where I had been
Or what was screened
The library of course
Deep dark secrets
Not to be shared
Until this day
Secret life far from
Ambitions of dad
Who liked to beat me
His son another doctor
Was not to be
Movies set me free
Mad youth lost in the dark
Try a little tenderness

Letters from the Edge

Do me a favor
When you die
Please send me an e-mail
I'm really curious
Did you see the white light
Was someone calling to you
The next evening
How about the yellow light
Bright and blinding
Coming forth by day
Tibetan Book of the Dead
Ever darker chromas
Terrifying demons
What are the odds
For a sinner like me
Breaking karmic cycle
Stray dog in the hood
Turned up recently
Could that be you
Or monkey in the zoo
Who do you hang with
So many celebrities
Perhaps an Elvis sighting
That's so cool
Wicked awesome
Green with envy
Well not really
Say hello to Larry
Oh how we miss him
So bye for now
Don't forget to write

Yesterday Today and Tomorrow

Today seems so like yesterday
Or tomorrow
The day after then after that
Or was stretching back
Forever and ever
Rolling and tumbling
Movius not my poet friend
Lord Geoffrey head of the cove
Master of tides
But Mobius stripped
Raw as birth
Nude and naked
Rude and lewd
Howling in the wind
Timeless quality of stark ether
Not taking a step
Forward or back
Total stasis
The is of what is
Now and forever
Amen to that brother
Right on mofo
Dis 'n' dat
Not here nor there
Where you at Big Boy
As Cardoso asked
Speedway hipster hovering over me
Back from Ibiza
Bogarting the joint as usual
So what else is new
Sheeeeet

Night Watch

Huddled 'round hearth
Circle of elders
Pulling close thick
Bearskin robes
His body strafed
Those massive claws
Fangs dug deep
Battered flesh
Furrowed map of
So many wounds
He recalled the day
When he died
Eons ago during
Winter in the woods
Cold and damp
Shivers of memory
Gazing down now
Sliver of light
Beam of energy
Warped time and space
Where yesterday
Morphs as tomorrow
Speck of eternity
A life reflected
Ever more difficult
Far more furrowed
With each incarnation
Braced against cold
Waning moon
Last of a clan
Deep in mind's eye

Gazing inward
Toward yet unborn
Wheel ever turning
The elder collapsed
Consumed by flames
First light when wolves howl

Cold Winter Night. Astrid Hiemer photo.

Jabberwocky

Taking dog for a walky
Dude from Milwaukee
Polish or German
Not that it matters
To y Mad Hatter
Dreams of hockey
Luck with y puck
Playoff time
Home ice it seems
For his team
Busting at y seams
So full of pride
Men at play
Y sports of boys
But then he cried
Gosh gazeeks
Heavens good grief
Behind by a goal
Sobbing buckets
Down on his luckish
Just reams and reams
Salted rivulets
Bathing his cheeks
Blithering bathos
Dog chimed in
Wooof woofing away
Night and day
Howled at y moon
Big ball of cheese
Luscious lunacy
Up in the sky

Far as y eye
Could see
Sea to bounding sea
Atlantic to Pistoffish
Not making waves
Jumping y sharks
Gentleman bent to scoop
Pooch's poop
Fresh and steamy
Brown and creamy
Back was stiff
Hip to me drift
Grunts and groans
Gave Bozo a bone
Must have decorum
Then oy oh boy
Score in overtime
Criminy caterwauling
Cats meowed
Choir of crickets
Utter cacophony
Ode to Joy
Jaunty cakewalk
Jabberwalking
Nonsense talking
With man's best friend
Gabba Gabba Hey
Slip sliding away

Highfalutin

Wading through
Pretentious stuff
Pundits pontificating
Yakking away
Night and day
Twists and turns
Over my head
Cosmic gonzology
Gobbledygook
By hook and crook
Up Cripple Creek
Way around the bend
Other people's money
Shop till you drop
Surfing the web
No stone unturned
Head pumping
Brain throbbing
What do I know
More than most perhaps
Ego and conceit
Less than many
Friggin nobody
Compared to few
Masters of the universe
Running their game
Moving the pieces
Pawns on a board
Checkers or chess
Keeping it simple
Just complicated enough

Make it interesting
Just you and me pal
Nothing but us chickens
End in sight
Season winding down
Soon summer reruns
Final cliffhanger
Series canceled
Not making sense
Your move mate
Endgame

Tethered Horse, Senegal. Astrid Hiemer photo.

Clean Coal

Air we breathe
Water we drink
Not just us
The whole world
Our entire planet
Not just America First
This land is your land
This land is my land
Bonkers out of hand
Paris Accord
Meaningful debate
Before it's too late
Nations agree
Except Syria
Not that surprising
Barrel bombing
Its own people
Nicaragua as well
Screed of hate
Now us too
More mean than meaningful
Bring back coal
Gulp, gasp, choke
Cripes no joke
The grim spin
Clean coal
Same old same old
Outlandish oxymoron
If you know what I mean
Falling apart
At the seams

Rabid mad dog
Snarling pit bull
Frothing at the mouth
Rants and raves
From his bully pulpit
Utter bullshit
Curse God and die

Icarus. Collage by Raeford Liles courtesy of the artist.

Mind Matters

What did you say
Sorry wasn't listening
Not that it matters
Mind over you know
Bit of this and that
Sameosameo
So it goes if
You catch the drift
From here to oblivion
When and if
Such a stiff
Bullshit
Matter of time
If you don't mind
But thanks anyway
You know what I mean
Perhaps not
Oh well what the hell
Here I be till then
Minding me P's and Q's
Whatever that means
Don't ask don't tell
Haven't a clue
Tough darts to you
The end is near
Oh my dear
Goodness gracious
I've nothing to wear
But fear itself
Another fine mess
You've gotten us into

Pass the carrot
I prefer a radish
Rubbish you say
Bloody bollocks
Godot only knows

Buddha Waterfall.

Salon

Engraved invitation
Dinner at the chateau
Like another time
So long ago
Centuries perhaps
Yet again
At the last minute
With nothing to wear
End of the table
Filling in for a
Marquis called off to war
Squeezed in between
Parish priest and local poet
Shabby guests
Like me it seems
Somewhat eccentric
Adding a dash of color
To social Siberia
Last night surprised
Moved up a few seats
Between bishop and rook
Across the table from
Aspiring politician
Now and then
Interjected with snarky remarks
Caught the gaze of our hostess
Elegant and cultured
Daring décolletage
Hushed little puppies
Snuggled in her bosom
Barking for nibbles
Tidbits of conversation
Delicious bon mots

Tossed in all directions
Lacking shape and form
Lively but chaotic
My head aswirl
Giddy as a girl
How we missed Voltaire
Called away it seems
So the countess said
Sucking on sorbet
Essence of raspberry
Between soup and duck
Before salad and cheese
When fate of world
Hung in balance
The general declaimed
Somewhat deranged
Senile it seems from
Shots to his head
Blessed by the bishop
Seeing an opening
Made a lame joke
Not very funny
They all laughed
Sang for my supper
Danse macabre
Gone with the wind
Until grim stranger
Ominous in dark cloth
Solemnly pronounced
End of Ancien Régime
Before mints and brandy
Teetering on oblivion
L'année dernière à Marienbad

Then and Now

If only I knew then
What I know now
How different it would be
No going back
Been there done that
What's next
The hear and now
More listening
Than saying
Never good at that
Always sounding off
Pontificating
Opinions on every subject
What critics do for a living
Sucking it all in
Spewed back
Mostly self absorbed
Not much reflection
Missing the irony
Of most moments
Called on it years later
Reputation cast in stone
Not really true
Nuanced by age
Worn down eroded
Boulders on the beach
Time softening
Hard body of youth
With brain to match
Bright as the sun
Thick as a brick

Evolving and eroding
All at once
Fighting against
Apathy and atrophy
An amusement for others
Revenge for insults
Real or imagined
Watching the old fart
Fall apart but not
Without a good fight

Heron. Astrid Hiemer photo.

Odyssey

What's to be done
Hard to say
We wake and work
Day by day
Mostly for others
Perhaps drudgery
The lucky ones
Artists and thinkers
Joy of self
Exquisite indulgence
Arguably the hardest
So difficult to define
Limitless imagination
Unchartered terrain
Vast oceans
Dense forests
Endless possibilities
Trudging on
One foot after another
Into that abyss
Ever deeper
Path leading on
No end in sight
Fork in the road
Taking it
An Odyssey
Journey home
From our war
Ending all wars
Youthful adventures
Romantic follies

Friends and enemies
Battered warriors
The fallen strewn
Dimly remembered
Now stumbled steps
No Virgil to guide us
Shades slipping past
Just before dawn
Long slanted shadows
First bright light
Sanguine horizon
Of another day
Staggering on and on

Procession of Maenads.

Cliffhanger

First scene of
The Oresteia
Ancient tragedy
High on a cliff
Above crashing waves
Wood piled high nearby
All those years
Others along the line
Far as the eye can see
Connecting dots
Signal fires
Lonely sentinels
Gazing out to sea
First to spot black ships
Back from ten-year war
So far away
Home hearths tended
Warmth to comfort warriors
Battered survivors
Legendary men
Endless vigil
Where and when
Gnawing why
Dimmed with time
A nation's ulcer
Rotting innards
Wives and sisters
Now rarely visit
Surging shore
Yearning for men
Gone long ago

Bent with age
Single mothers
Their dimmed torches
Burning less brightly
Because of that whore
Vile widow-maker

For Whom the Bell Tolls. Astrid Hiemer photo.

Pinball Wizard

Thinking of me
As a bubble
Self as molecule
Center surrounded
Shaped by jelly
Within symmetrical
Clear membrane
Single cell organism
When in harmony
A smooth sphere
Floating in ambient space
Air and sky
Perhaps water
Wafted by stream and tide
River or brook
Vast oceans
Space both inner and outer
When all is well
Even pressure
Balance of entropy
A perfect ball
Balance of opposites
When stressed
Pressure tests
Distorted shapes
Gentle ellipse at best
Or crusted and cratered
Lunar surface
Bombarded by meteors
Smashing into that me
Or violent eruptions

Breaking out
Crashing against outer membrane
No longer a rolling ball
Smoothly navigating
Roiled and rocked
Slammed about
Psychic cyclotron
Bumpy ride
Other as pinball wizard
Menacing presence
Manipulating flippers
Flashing lights
Running up scores
Someone else's game
When life is not exactly
A silver ball

On the Rocks.

Hill of Beans

What's that mean
A hill of beans
Is it the beans
Or the hill
Ain't much of nuthin
So it seems
Most folks pokin' bout
Don't mount to much
Punchin' the clock
Here and there
Now to then
Not much Zen
In them thar hills
Beans is good fer yah
Fullah protein
Keeps yah goin'
Truth be told
Ketchup and hot sauce
Real tasty like
Gives you gas
Ain't so bad
Right nice fartin' some
Makes folks mad
Seems kindah sad
Working up a nice
Head of steam
Crackin' one
Cept in elevators
Gets yah all shot up
Drug off tuh
Boot Hill

Gun slingers
Bad hombres
Stone-cold killers
Piled up yay high
Reachin' for the sky
Autah be a law
Ginst beans and such
Offends city folks
OK mungst us pokes
Cuttin' some SBDs
Them's no joke

Lisbon Beans.

Eternity.com

Pharaoh yawned
Time for tea
Snacks fit for a king
End of another day
Ruling two lands
Upper and Lower Egypt
Even that gets old
Samosamo
Like anything else
Not as much fun
As it used to be
When daddy died
Such a stiff
Putting him to rest
What an ordeal
Starting his own funeral
Too many details
No more friggin' pyramids
So damned expensive
All that rock piled up
Yesterday another trip
Sweltering desert
Dry and dusty
Valley of the Kings
Middle of nowhere
Seeing how things
Were coming along
Chambers for the queens
Then the kids
Each demanding a
Room of their own

Glad when it's over
Finally eternal rest
Some peace and quiet
Richly deserved
No more headaches
Hittites and Nubians
Who needs the aggravation
Wives constant bickering
Yak yak yak
Day and night
Yaddayaddayadda
Looking forward to being
Praise the gods
Now and forever
An exquisite corpse

Egyptian Fayum Mummy Portrait.

Time Flies

Zoom
Rushing by in a blur
Seemingly ever faster
More urgent now
Than when I was young
Horny and stoned
Hellhound on my heels
Keeping a step ahead
Checking the clock
How much time left
We ask in a frantic
Race without winners
Crossing the finished line
So much to get done
What happened today
Just came and went
Whoooosh
Followed by the
Grim evening news
So many plans
Now hastened
Cutting no slack
For ephemera
Trite and trivial
Shifted priorities
Finishing books
Planning exhibitions
Serious stuff
No sitting by the beach
Screw the snowbirds
Their endless sunsets

Waiting for tide to roll in
Framed by palm trees
More like bracing for
Tsunami washing
Us all to Kingdom
Come or Kong
Gorilla in the room
Hear the roar

Withered Stump. Astrid Hiemer photo.

Fear Eats Itself

What is the fear
I feel more and more
Eating away at me
Inside down deep
The unsettling
Inching along
Relentless unease
Perhaps you too
Much unrest
Nightly sleep
Not what it was
Creeping to the edge
Crab crossing sand
Dragging a groove
Dung beetle
Rolling its ball
Ever to the sun
Scarabs in Egypt
Where Pyramids endure
Markers of time
Ever more eroded
Counting the waves
Edge of oceans
Pounding surf
Gnawing uncertainty
Quoth the Raven, Evermore
Today dear friend
Immense Larry
Girth and mirth
Read your obituary
In the Eagle

Life in too few lines
Instead of flowers
I send you this

View of Toledo.

Punctuation

Where to put the commas
Here, there, everywhere
Perhaps none at all
Screw it to syntax
Poetic license
Smashmouth flow
Face jamming
Cheek to jowl
Assault on senses
Staccato onslaught
Hammered away
Heat oppressed
Brain on steroids
Reach back and
Punt end-over-end
Mile high floater
Red zone
Goal line stand
Rush to judgment
Going for the gold
Feel the burn
Lap dancing
Pole vaulting
Showing pink
Naughty but nice
Cutting a slice
Down and dirty
Laying rubber
Zoom zoom
See you later
After awhile

Crocodile
Who was that
Masked man
With no friggin'
Common sense or
Decent punctuation

Fence Rockport. Astrid Hiemer photo.

You Be Cool Man

Yo hey guy
Say Dude
That be you mutah
Whaz happening
Where you at man
What be goin' on
You hep to the jive
Laying down
Tail on some frails
Got eyes on it
Copping some smoke
On the corner
Down the hood
Packing heat
Like I was saying
Know what I mean
Fucked up man
Me and Julio
Was in the crib
Cut out
Took a stroll
He be fresh
New kicks
So fly man
Rolled the bones
It be bad man
Split the scene
Off the hook
Them bulls
Be mean man
Know what I mean

Shit going down
Crazy man
Mutthahfuggah
Like I was saying
Cut out
Split man
Scene was smoked
Know what I mean
Later man
You be cool
Shit getting heavy
Like I was saying
Ya'll fall by
Hang with the bros
Lay back
Do some blow
Like I was saying
Man

Bloom. Astrid Hiemer photo.

Quotidian

Here and now
Quotidian
Such intensity
Seemingly ordinary
Assault on senses
Exacerbating media
Bloviating President
No big deal
In vast scheme
Blip on radar
Brief candle
That stage of life
Stretching back
Chemical soup
Before the bang
Where was God
Before the before
Unavoidable void
Space and time
Being and nothingness
Non-Newtonian
Just entropy
The present
Midpoint to
Oblivion
When night sky
Goes dark
Stars burned out
Energy depleted
Inevitable
Where was I

Before God
The prophets
Philosophers
Emperors
All vanity
Only entropy
Dancing along
Yellow brick road
Delusions of meaning
What's for dinner
Call me Ishmael

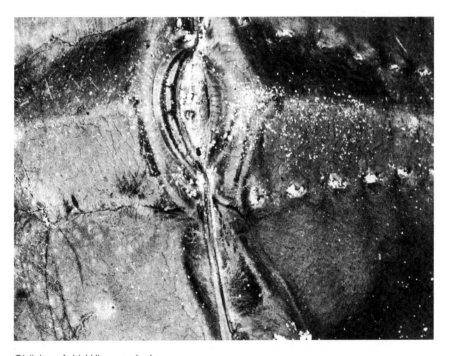

Oblivion. Astrid Hiemer photo.

Journey

Blank canvas
Make a mark
Then another
Initial idea
Work emerges
Finished for now
Contemplated
Mulled over
Muse reconsidered
Another start
Fresh take
Reaching similar
Conclusion
Not satisfactory
Feeding on itself
Branches off
Hacking passage
Dense obstacles
Focus refined
Detritus along
Road to oasis
Under date palms
Cool water
Reflective rest
Moving on
Artist evolves

New Histories

Some time back
Lunch with
Long lost friend
Shared memories
Nostalgia for times
Long gone
Good laughs
But I said
Remaining friends
Means
Creating new
Histories
Without which
No reason
To meet more often than
Chance encounters
At parties or funerals

Pipe Dream

Deep winter sleep
Nary a peep
Tweet, tweet, tweet
Tweaks of Spring
Meet and Magritte
This is not a pipe
Why the heck not
Tossing about
To and fro
So it goes bro
Slip and slide
Glide through night
Pro and con
Here and gone
Gone baby gone
Grand Gonfalon
Pennant fever
Sprigs of summer
Spring training
Just days away
Hip hip hurray
So what's with the
Friggin' pipe
Sure looks like one
Come dawn it seems
Wafting in dreams
Up in smoke
Wacko joke
That Belgian bloke
Taking a toke
Lonesome cowpoke

Singing away
Yippie-ki-yay
Here comes day

Mesa.

Grounded

Lunch in Pittsfield
We talked with melancholy
Grounded after 26 years
End of blue sky
That flight we took
Not so long ago
Looking down edge of abyss
Where all have been
That moment in every life
So much art, poetry
Religion and philosophy
Each in our own way
Not one like any other
Different as snowflakes
All other experiences
Not overshadow our own
Dance on precipice
Sleep perchance to dream
Absurdly to wax poetic
Make of it anguished art
You scoffed at that
Such arrogance of self
How dare to speak the unknowable
Defy the rites
Up yours to priests
Curse God and die
Shun smells and bells
Ashes to ashes
Ultimate dust off
Not stand mute as all others
Death a fact not contest

Age a gradual demise
Sobering reality of decline
Mostly gone you said
Ever more precious
Daily increment of what was
Not yet no more but
Ever less it seems
Can I tie my shoe
Come sit by me
Here upon the ground
Still wet with spring
Let us talk of kings
Falling like reign
Not an epic like Dante's
Perhaps a slight moment
An intimate comment on
All that was and will be
Our meager middle passage
The merest blip
Tree dropping in dense forest
Uttering its sound
Falling with a thud
Heard by none
Possibly a few
Maybe me and you
A word or two
Uttered in eulogy
Into the ether
Thin vapor of memory
Wafting forever and ever
Space is the place

The Skinny

Entering the room
A lively gathering
One kind or other
Drinks and snacks
Folks milling about
Chirps of chatter
Chips and dips
The usual small talk
Veneer of power and privilege
Sense of entitlement
Just being there
Among the hoi polloi
Smug sense of belonging
Or perhaps not
Raised as an orphan
By busy parents
As I told Jose
The other day at lunch
Too much but never enough
Reading, writing, 'rithmetic
Like in the robing room
Before annual convocation
Ho hum university
Anywhere USA
Penguin Island
Swell of Orwellian
Strutting about
Parades of professors
Hoods and hats
Blue for Yale
Oxford or Cambridge

Red for Harvard
On such occasions
Looking about for
Someone like me
Straight old white guys
Their proper wives
Wrinkled gracefully
Sipping oaky chardonnay
Milk of the masses
Sherry before supper
Country club stuff
My winter of Chianti
Cheap and potable
Like me déclassé
Opaquely Italian
Not quite white
Enough for refined company
What's worse Sicilian
A made-up man
Mob psychology
Gangster chic
The other half not
Thick and stumpy
From peasant stock
Lived on potatoes
Working the sod
Emerald Island
Dublin with stout
Celebrated my birthday
Such a merry night
Music and mirth

Astrid dancing about
Knocking back black pints
Feeling the Mick in me
Blarney gift of gab
How to make sense
Born in the U.S.A.
Such roiling of race
Burn baby burn
Ranked and filed
Rooted into us
From birth in a land
Diverse with girth
Fly in the buttermilk
He says with a laugh
Making light of the horror
The horror, the horror
Kurtz in the cave
Piles of little arms
Okinawa, Korea, Vietnam, Iraq, Afghanistan
Boots on the ground
Old men make wars
Slaughter our children
Now Assad and Syria
Mission accomplished
Tweeted Commander in Sleeze
Corpses of Wounded Knee
Scent of magnolia
The gallant south
Black bodies hung from poplar trees
Custer died for your sins
Gone with the wind

Lillian my black mother
Listened to joy and pain
Cookies after school
Growing up absurd
Nausea of that room
Any time anywhere
Where everyone looks alike
Even jazz clubs
Miles, Mingus and Trane
Played with love supreme
Heart and soul
For ofay hipsters
At least on the outside
Heart of darkness
Rage and turmoil
Nausea of small talk
Seeking deeper dialogues
Why race matters
In the DNA of
Being an American
Where nothing is as it seems
Women walking to and fro
Speaking of Michelangelo
For tough shit Eliot
One of the better Italians

Big Foot

Oh to be well shod
Not some friggin' clod
Wacko clodhopper
Ain't hip to the jive
Clomping on sod
Clog dancing
Clink clanking in barns
Smiles of a summer night
Romps in the hay
Two backed straw dogs
Unstuffed scarecrows
Raggedy Anns flopping about
Amos and Andy
When they were funny
So many shoes in my closet
Dozens of pairs
Fit for all occasions
From Beatle Boots to clogs
Them what was copped in Copenhagen
When I knocked back schnapps
Lunch with hipster Dexter Gordon
Acid flashbacks to
Summer of 1968
Strawberry pink kicks
Purple pimp suits
Living in the ghetto
Fort Hill Roxbury
Looking fresh
When it seemed to matter
More flash than substance
Living outside the law

Urban cowboy
High noon on mean streets
Shoe in for mayhem
Street fighting man
Signed, sealed, delivered
Swathed in Purple Haze
A half century on
Hoist the gonfalon
Now just two pairs
Stout ones for winter
Slosh of Berkshire slush
Summer Topsiders
Like rotating tires
Gottah have wheels man
Groovin' on down the road
Highway to hell and back
Stairway to heaven
Where angels go barefoot
There ain't no mirrors
All is vanity
Slip sliding sanity
Long and winding road
Fab Four no more
I am the walrus

Foucault You Man

As in Magritte's
Ceci n'est pas une pipe
Le dernier cri
Beware of Geeks bearing gifts
This is not a poem
Not written by me
Author-wise so it seems
Lacks authorenticity
Superannuated individuality
Not owner but liable
Sued yet not acknowledged
Such a kvetch
Ambiguities of ownership
Shakespeare or Bacon
Explication de texte
École normale supérieure
To which one does not apply
Confluence of ideas
Lacking in originality
The fictive Homer
Name branding a bunch of stuff
Not even consistent
Illiad differs from Odyssey
Or four Evangelists
Myth of sacred words
The Prophet Muhammad
Not author of Koran
Infallible text passed through him
Dictated by angel Gabriel
Perhaps this poem disseminates
Recontextualizing like
Aristotle, Marx or Freud

Less authors than concepts
Death to authors
Killed as by Nietzsche
Dead poets society
Hegemonic canon of white guys
Casualties of Intersectionality
Archaic cult of personality
Romance of literature
Skeletal old boy friends
Byron, Keats and Shelley
Perhaps even Whitman and Eliot
Marginalia of rabbis and monks
Comments on comments on comments
Threads in Facebook
Blood of the poets
Ersatz Talmudic traditions
As if we count as well
Grand scheme of things
Foucault you man
Don't you mean fuck you
No baby Foucault
Then again who am I to say
Post-structuralism word play
Thoughts for another day
Here today gone tomorrow
Author author
Yet another standing O
For nobody of note
Theatre of the absurd
Back to Beckett
Tomorrow never comes

For Jane and Robert

Made in the USA
Middletown, DE
11 February 2019